I Didn't Need To Know That

Mícheál O Fiachra

DEDICATION

I would like to thank Catherine MacHale Gunnarsson for helping me with the editing, Clinton Laverty for help with editing and pushing me to finish it in a non nagging way, and especially Marta Suchan.

Linux Official Mascot

The official Linux mascot is a penguin because its creator Linus Torvalds was once bitten by a Little Penguin (Eudyptula minor).

Fish can drown in water

Fish can drown in water as they don't actually breathe water but instead filter out the oxygen, and if the water isn't sufficiently aerated, they will asphyxiate.

Long Sleep

Snails can sleep for up to three years if the climatic situation is not suitable for them to thrive. This process is called estivation.

Charlie Chaplin

The actor and comedian Charlie Chaplin once entered a Charlie Chaplin look-alike contest and lost.

Candy Floss

One of the inventors of candy floss was a dentist.

Slogan competitions

One of the reasons that companies run slogan competitions is that by constructing the slogan, the person entering the competition convinces themselves that the product is desirable or has value. Hence, in a sense, they are advertising the product to themselves.

Propeller

The largest (cargo ship) propellers are the ones used on the Maersk Line's Triple-E Class. They weigh over 70 tonnes with a diameter of over 10 metres. Casting each one takes just 10 minutes but takes over 10 days to cool.

Hitler's brother

Adolf Hitler had a half brother Alois. He worked briefly in the Shelbourne Hotel in Dublin until his arrest for theft in 1900 for which he served a five-month sentence. He had two sons William and Heinz.

Alert, Canada

The small village of Alert lies on the northernmost part of the Nunavut territory in Canada. Located just over 800 kms from the North Pole, it is the northernmost regularly inhabited place in the world. Due to its remote geographic location it is one of the most dangerous, and inhospitable places to live in the world.

Brain freeze

The medical term for a brain freeze is sphenopalatine ganglioneuralgia. This headache is caused by the consumption of cold drinks or food stuffs.

Winston Churchill

Along with being a legendary statesman, Winston Churchill was also an accomplished and prolific author, and he won the Nobel Prize in Literature in 1953 for his historical writings.

Indeed, much of Churchill's income was made from writing books and articles for newspapers and magazines, as Members of Parliament were paid only a nominal salary up to 1946 and he needed to support himself.

Bus Lane Benefits

One of the unintended but welcome side effects of introducing bus lanes is the increased cardiac arrest survival rate due to ambulances being able to get to patients and to hospitals faster.

Lamborghini

Ferruccio Lamborghini founded a tractor company Lamborghini Trattori S.p.A, which became one of the largest agricultural equipment manufacturers in Italy. Ferruccio Lamborghini celebrated his success by buying a Ferrari. The clutch on his Ferrari failed and he discovered that the clutch on his Ferrari was exactly the same clutch that he used to manufacture his tractors. Lamborghini went to Ferrari and asked for a better replacement. Ferrari responded, saying that he was just a tractor maker, and could not know anything about sports cars. This snub was the inspiration that lead Lamborghini to pursue an automobile manufacturing venture with the goal of bringing to life his vision of a perfect grand tourer.

Amazon

John Wainwright was Amazon's first customer. He purchased Hofstadter's *Fluid Concepts and Creative Analogies: Computer Models of the Fundamental Mechanisms of Thought* on April 3rd, 1995 and since then Amazon named a building after him.

Amazon was originally to be called Relentless and can still be accessed via the relentless.com URL.

Amazon's logo includes an arrow going from the A to the Z.

Bell Labs

Bell Labs was the research and development arm of AT&T and the Western Electric Company. Bell Labs' researchers research lead to the development of radio astronomy, the transistor, the laser, the charge-coupled device, information theory, the UNIX operating system, the C programming language, S programming language and the C++ programming language.

Radioactive notebooks

The pioneering Polish scientist Marie Skłodowska-Curie was the first woman to win the Nobel prize. She won it in 1906 in conjunction with her husband Pierre Curie and Henri Becquerel, for their work on radioactivity. She later became the first scientist to win two Nobel prizes when she won it again in 1911. She named the first chemical element that she discovered - polonium - after her native country Poland. She also coined the term radioactivity. An interesting legacy of her work is that her own notebooks are to this day still radioactive.

A Muntin

The strip separating window panes is called a muntin.

East versus West

The division between the former East and West Berlin can still be seen by night from air or space due to the different bulbs used in the street lights.

Odd places to stay around the world

The Giraffe Manor in Nairobi, Kenya is famous for its resident herd of Rothschild Giraffe, which you can find at the breakfast table, the front door and even your bedroom window.

The Mirrorcube in Harads, Sweden, is a lightweight aluminium 4m x 4m x 4m box suspended around a tree trunk and covered in mirrors. It is accessed by means of a rope bridge.

China's Tianjin Aircraft Carrier Hotel located at Bagua is a former Soviet aircraft carrier built in 1970 as the Kiev.

Capsule hotels are an innovation that developed in Japan. They provide cheap accommodation for guests whose primary concern is just sleeping. They are particularly suited to revellers who miss the last train home.

It is possible to stay in several different lighthouses in Britain and Ireland as they are available to rent through the National Trusts in both countries.

Every winter for the last 25 years from the beginning of December it has been possible to stay in an Ice Hotel in the small town of Jukkasjärvi, Sweden. And though it is constructed entirely from snow and ice it is required to have a fire alarm!

Tattoo taboo

In Japan tattoos are associated with organised crime.

Corpse cupboards

Some airlines have corpse cupboards fitted in their planes for passengers that die on board.

The day after tomorrow

There is a specific word for the day after tomorrow in English: overmorrow from the Middle English *overmorwe*.

Richest cities

The world's five richest cities are London, Los Angeles, New York, Tokyo and Seoul.

TV goldmine

The .tv domain name has proved to be a gold mine for the tiny island nation of Tuvalu located in the Pacific Ocean. The Tuvalu government receives royalties for use of the country's domain name, which is used for television show websites and related industries.

Lego

The name Lego is a combination of two Danish words, "leg godt", which means "play well".

Lego started when carpenter Ole Kirk Christiansen started making wooden toys, a few years later he bought Denmark's first injection moulding machine, and began experimenting with cellulose acetate construction blocks. His son Godtfred perfected the design and switched to another even more durable plastic, acrylonitrile butadiene styrene.

Lego is the largest manufacturer of tyres (albeit small ones) in the world.

A niche area of investing has grown up around Lego. The investment activities include buying sets and holding them until they are discontinued and the price rises, "part out" which is selling parts like mini figures that command high prices and finally arbitrage (buying from countries where they sell for lower prices and selling them where they command higher prices). And if the worst comes to the worst one can always play (well) with your investment!

Velcro

Velcro is a trademark for a technology called "hoop and loop". Hoop and loop's originated in 1941 when a Swiss engineer was looking at why burrs stuck to him and his dog after a walk in the countryside. Velcro is so named for the combination of the French words *velours* and *crochet*.

Esperanto

Esperanto is the most widely spoken artificial language. It was created by L. L. Zamenhof with the intention of fostering peace and understanding between people with different languages. However, it has been supplanted by English as a lingua franca.

US Interstate Road System

Contrary to popular belief, Interstate highways don't have one mile straight in every five miles to act as a landing strip but they do have a military role as they form part of the Strategic Highway Network, a system of roads identified as critical to the US Department of Defense.

The US Interstate System owes its existence to Eisenhower's first-hand experience of Germany's Reichsautobahn during World War 2 and his involvement in a simulation of a 3-mile-long army convoy traversing the US. It averaged a dismal 6 mph coast to coast. This experience lead to his championing the cause of the Interstate Road System.

Nowadays it is possible to drive coast to coast in under 29 hours, a feat recently accomplished in a specially modified Mercedes CL55 AMG.

Alaska, Hawaii, and Puerto Rico all have roads that make up part of the Interstate road network despite not having direct land connections to other states.

Interstates routes with odd numbers run north and south, while the even numbered ones run east and west.

The longest Interstate route is approximately 3,020 miles and runs from Seattle Washington to Boston Massachusetts.

The US Interstate System has now been surpassed in length by the Chinese system.

Mail Rail

In 1927 the Royal Mail opened a driverless rail system between East London, Mount Pleasant and Paddington, which took a quarter of London's postal traffic off the streets. It was eventually closed in 2003.

Santa Claus

The United Kingdom's Royal Mail has a team that answers letters addressed to Santa Claus.

Space Shuttle

The 5 space shuttles were called Atlantis, Challenger, Columbia, Discovery and Endeavour.

Astronaut Story Musgrave holds the distinction of being the only astronaut to fly on all five space shuttles.

One launch of the space shuttle Discovery was delayed due to woodpeckers pecking at the insulation.

The hottest temperature reached by the exterior of the shuttle on re-entry was 1650 degrees centigrade.

The first space shuttle astronauts, John W. Young and Robert L. Crippen, asked for M&M's to be included in the food supply for the two-day, record-setting earth orbit.

Punctuality

In Japan trains are generally so punctual that when one is on the rare occasion late one can get a special slip from the stationmaster to give to your workplace to explain that you were late because the train was delayed.

Panama Canal

Richard Halliburton the explorer paid a toll of 36 cents to swim the length of the Panama Canal.

Lethal weapon

Karate black belts above 4th Dan have to register at police stations in Japan.

Benford's law

Benford's Law relates to the frequency of distribution of digits in real-life data. Examples include utility bills, stock prices, lengths of rivers, expense report receipts, etc.

According to Benford's Law, the number 1 occurs as the leading digit circa 30% of the time, while larger numbers occur in that position less frequently with the number 9 appearing as the first digit less than 5% of the time.

Benford's Law also concerns the expected distribution for digits beyond the first, which approach a uniform distribution.

This can be used in a business context to detect accounting and expense form fraud by comparing the expected first and subsequent digit distribution as expected by Benford's Law and those in examples submitted by fraudsters who are not aware of the existence or practical applications of Benford's Law.

Saturn V

The Saturn V, at 111 meters tall and weighing in at 2,800 metric tonnes, was the most powerful rocket flown and was used in the Apollo and Skylab space programmes.

The power output from the Saturn V first stage engine was 60 gigawatts, which is roughly the same as the peak electricity demand of a country the size of the United Kingdom.

Jeff Bezos funded a successful salvage attempt to recover F1 engine Number 5 used in the Apollo 11 moon-landing mission. It was jettisoned shortly after lift-off into the Atlantic sea where it lay until it was found 44 years later.

A team of NASA engineers dismantled a F-1 engine in an effort to understand how it operated and potentially use the information to build a new variant F-1B, which could be used in modern space exploration.

Modern Moon Landing

The question is often asked: "Could we fly to the moon today?" The answer is: Not straight away, as much of the infrastructure was dismantled and key skills forgotten.

Apartheid

The pencil test was a method of assessing whether a person had Afro-textured hair and was used as a test for race under the apartheid regime in South Africa. A pencil is pushed through a person's hair, how easily it comes out determines whether the person has "passed" or "failed" the test.

Intelligent electrical network

Major industrial users of electricity such as aluminium smelters often have load-balancing deals with electrical utilities in exchange for reduced power billing rates. If the grid frequency drops below a certain level, the user will limit its own power consumption to compensate for the supply shortfall. The user detects from the grid frequency itself that the adjustment is required so no intervention is required by the utility.

Living in the past

Experiments have shown that the lag between things happening and us experiencing them is about 80 milliseconds.

PIN security

In data condensed from released/exposed/discovered password tables and security breaches, it was found that over 10% of 4-digit PIN numbers were 1234 and the top 20 choices made up over 25% of PINs. 2580 features high on the list as it is all the numbers in the centre of a phone keypad from top to bottom.

Nuclear missile launch codes

The secret launch code for the United States Minuteman nuclear missiles was set at 00000000 for over 20 years. Originally mandated as a safeguard by the Defense secretary, this intent was overridden by the Strategic Air Command, which immediately had them all set to all zeros, and this was even included in their printed standard operating procedures.

Canary in a coal mine

Coal mines are hazardous working environments due to the presence of toxic gases such carbon monoxide, carbon dioxide or methane.

As early mines did not have sophisticated ventilation systems or gas detection systems like modern mines the effects of these toxic gases could be catastrophic.

Canaries are especially sensitive to methane and carbon monoxide, and any signs of distress shown by a canary served as a warning of a build-up of these dangerous gases.

This is where the expression "Canary in a coal mine" came from.

The last 200 coal mine canaries in the United Kingdom were made redundant in 1986, ending a tradition that dated back to 1911.

Largest submarine

The Russian Akula or Shark class submarine with the NATO reporting name of Typhoon is a type of nuclear-powered ballistic missile submarine first deployed by the Soviet Navy in the 1980s. With a submerged displacement of 48,000 tons, the Typhoon class were the largest submarines ever built.

Jingoistic

Of the almost 193 current member states of the United Nations, the British have by some accounts, at some point in history, invaded, had some control of or established a military presence in 171 of them.

One country

Finland is separated by only one country (Russia) from North Korea.

Children's beer

In the Middle Ages, beers with a very low alcohol content were commonly consumed as a safer alternative to untreated water as the alcohol killed many common pathogens. Even children consumed these beers.

Barrel of Oil

A barrel of oil, which is abbreviated as bbl is defined as 42 US gallons in both Canada and the United States. This size originated in the early Pennsylvania oil fields. This anachronistic measure is still used today to quote prices of various oil benchmarks such as Brent Crude or West Texas Intermediate.

BLEVE

A boiling liquid expanding vapour explosion or BLEVE is an explosion caused by the rupture of a vessel containing a pressurised liquid above its boiling point. The liquid and vapour ignite and cause an explosion.

Tragedy of the commons

The tragedy of the commons is the depletion of a group resource by individuals who act independently and rationally solely in their own interest but with the understanding that depleting the common resource is contrary to the group's long-term best interests. This dilemma was first explored by ecologist Garrett Hardin in his seminal paper in the journal *Science*.

Wildlife bridges

Banff National Park in Alberta, Canada built 24 bridges specifically for wildlife. The bridges are wide and covered with vegetation to encourage animals to use them. It is reported that up to 10 large mammal species have used the bridges in the past 25 years.

The Mad Hatter

Historically hat makers were exposed to mercuric nitrate, which was used as part of the process of curing felt in the hat-making process. This continual exposure by contact through their hands and by breathing in the toxic fumes often led to mercury poisoning. One of the common symptoms of mercury poisoning is insanity. This phenomenon was the inspiration for the Lewis Carroll character the Mad Hatter in *Alice in Wonderland.*

Tulipomania

Tulipomania was the name given to a point in Dutch history when prices of the recently introduced tulip bulb reached extremely high levels and then just as suddenly collapsed. At the peak of Tulipomania in 1637 some tulip bulbs sold for more than the price of a house. It is generally considered to be the first recorded speculative bubble (or economic bubble).

The Pentagon

The Pentagon is the headquarters of the United States Department of Defense and is located in Arlington County, Virginia.

It has 17.5 miles of corridors and 6.5 million square feet of offices.

Despite its large size it is possible to walk to anywhere else in the Pentagon in approximately 7 minutes.

The Pentagon has twice the number of toilet facilities needed for a building of its size due to providing racially separate toilets as per the state of Virginia's racial laws at the time of it's construction.

The design chosen was based on minimising the amount of steel used in its construction due to steel shortages during World War 2.

Soviet Russia targeted a small building in the centre of the Pentagon figuring that the building must be very strategically important if it is protected by 5 giant walls. It is in fact a hot dog stand!

In 2012 the U.S. defence budget was more than $682 billion, which was more than the defence spending of the next 10 top spending countries combined.

Gmail

Google announced Gmail to the public on April 1, 2004 and because if its generous (at the time) size limit (1 GB of free space) many people thought it was actually an April Fools' Day joke rather than a serious endeavour.

Google bought the Gmail.com domain from Garfield.com. Garfield.com originally used it as part of their free email service.

John Harvey Kellogg

John Harvey and Will Keith Kellogg invented cornflakes. The brothers disagreed over the question of adding sugar to cereals so they went their separate ways. Will Keith set up Battle Creek Toasted Corn Flake Company while John Harvey continued with the Kellogg name, which has survived to this day. Rice Krispies were added to the product line in 1928.

White chocolate

White chocolate contains no actual chocolate (cocoa solids or chocolate liqueur)!

Easter Eggs

An Easter Egg is an intentional inside joke, hidden message, or feature in a creative work such as a computer program, movie, book, or crossword.

The 1997 version of Microsoft Office featured a hidden flight simulator in Microsoft Excel and a pinball game in Microsoft Word.

The Google search product includes a number of Easter eggs that can be found when certain words are used as search terms:

tilt - the results are displayed at an angle
recursion - the user is asked did they mean to search for recursion
do a barrel roll - this is an homage to the Nintendo game Star Fox 64

Google Maps includes a number of Easter eggs that can be found when certain directions are sought.

Searching for walking directions from the Shire to Mordor produces "One does not simply walk into Mordor", a warning that replicates a line from The Lord of the Rings.

Politicians with high IQs

Arnold Schwarzenegger is reputed to have an IQ of 135 and Hillary Clinton reputedly has a higher IQ than Bill Clinton.

Mea Culpa

Mea culpa translates as through my fault; the modern equivalent is my bad.

Lethologica

Lethologica describes the inability to remember words, phrases or names.

Bentley

Ian Fleming's James Bond originally drove a Bentley rather than an Aston Martin.

Nightmare

The word nightmare is derived from the Old English *mære*, a Germanic folkloric goblin who rode on people's chests as they slept.

Ghoti

Ghoti is a constructed word used to illustrate irregularities in the spelling of words in the English language

Though spelt as ghoti, it can be pronounced as fish as follows: the gh as in tough, the o as in women and the ti as in nation

Jehovah's Witnesses

Jehovah's Witnesses were originally a book distribution workforce for author Charles Russell in the late 1800s.

Bubonic plague

Bubonic plague was responsible for the deaths of a third of Europe's population in the Middle Ages. There are still occurrences of it in parts of Africa. Bubonic plague is caused by the *Yersinia pestis* bacterium, which is usually transmitted through the bite of an infected rat flea. An outbreak in Madagascar in December 2013 killed 32 people.

Federal Helium Reserve

The United States has a National Helium Reserve at the Cliffside Storage Facility in Texas containing over 1 billion cubic meters of helium gas. The reserve was first established in 1925 as a strategic supply of gas for airships, but subsequently in the 1950s became an important source of coolant required for the Space program.

Fast-food restaurants

Fast food restaurants make use of the fact that people are more likely to eat faster and spend less time at the table if the restaurant is loud.

Similarly, the seats are uncomfortable so as to discourage patrons from lingering too long.

They make larger size options as they found customers were less embarrassed to ask for a larger size than an extra helping.

Many accept credit cards because they find people will spend more on average using a credit card than paying cash.

Guinness Book of Records

The Guinness Book of Records was originally published by Guinness Breweries as a reference for settling bar arguments.

Collective nouns

Collective nouns date back to an English hunting tradition of the late Middle Ages.

Some of the more interesting ones include:

Ladybirds - loveliness
Crows - murder
Flamingos - flamboyance
Owls - parliament
Ferrets- business
Ravens - unkindness or conspiracy
Hedgehogs - prickle
Kittens - kindle

Pink Flamingo

Flamingos are pink because they eat brine shrimp or blue-green algae, which contains beta carotene, the same compound that makes carrots orange. In zoos they need to be fed beta-carotene or canthaxanthin so as to retain their pink colour.

Passports

One can travel to up to 173 countries without a visa on a UK or Finnish passport.

Rolls-Royce cars

Rolls-Royce Limited was founded by Charles Stewart Rolls and Sir Frederick Henry Royce on 15 March 1906.

Rolls-Royce doesn't use cowhide for its seats because of concerns that female cattle are prone to getting stretch marks during pregnancy so instead it uses the hide of 15 to 18 Bavarian bulls per car.

Rolls-Royce cars don't break down: they fail to proceed.

The majority of all the Rolls-Royce cars ever made are still on the road to day.

The hood ornament is called The Spirit of Ecstasy and nowadays retracts automatically in the event of an accident.

The company, which had both an aeronautical and a motoring arm, split into Rolls-Royce plc and Rolls-Royce Motors in 1973.

Charles Rolls was killed at Bournemouth in July 1910 becoming the first person to die in a British air accident.

Merlin Engine

The Merlin is a British liquid-cooled, 27 Litre V-12, piston aero engine most famous for powering the legendary Spitfire.

It is named after the bird of prey rather than the wizard.

A detuned version of the V12 supercharged Merlin engine that powered the Spitfire fighter was used to power the Centurion tank.

The Merlin was Henry Royce's last aero engine design.

Insanity

Insanity is not a medical term but instead a legal term that refers to a criminal defendant's ability to distinguish right from wrong at the time he allegedly committed a crime.

The idea of pleading insanity as a criminal defence was first established in 16th-century England.

Sealand

The Principality of Sealand is located on HM Fort Roughs, a former Second World War Maunsell Sea Fort. This is located in the North Sea, 13 kilometres (7 nautical miles) off the coast of Suffolk, England, United Kingdom.

Sealand lays claim to being world's smallest nation but is not currently officially recognised by any other established sovereign state.

It was first occupied in 1967 by Paddy Roy Bates, who seized it from a group of pirate radio broadcasters. At first he intended to set up his own pirate radio station but in 1975 he established Sealand as a nation when he wrote a constitution and established other national symbols.

Bates moved to mainland Essex when he became elderly and named his son Michael Regent of Sealand in his place.

An English court ruling that the court did not have jurisdiction over Sealand is about as far as it goes in terms of international recognition.

Thane of Cawdor

Shakespeare's play Macbeth features a fictional character called the Thane of Cawdor but there is also a real life Thane of Cawdor.

M&M's

Forrest Mars was in Spain during the Civil War there and he saw soldiers eating chocolate pellets called Smarties, which had a hard shell of tempered chocolate surrounding an inner piece of chocolate. He created his own copy and called them M&M's. M&M's were particularly suited for inclusion in military rations due to their ability to withstand extremes of temperatures.

The two "Ms" represent the names of Forrest E. Mars Sr., the founder of Newark Company, and Bruce Murrie, son of Hershey Chocolate's president William F. R. Murrie

ZZ Top

ZZ Top drummer Frank Beard is, ironically, the only member of the band not to have a beard.

Formula 1

Formula 1 cars are made up of approximately 80,000 components.

Formula 1 cars generate so much down force that they could in theory drive upside down.

When braking, a Formula 1 driver will experience over 5g of g-force on his body (that's a force of load five times a driver's own bodyweight), and as much as 4g while cornering.

A Formula One car can go from 0 to km/h mph in 1.5 seconds.

Over a Formula 1 race weekend a driver will change gear about 8,000 times.

Though Formula 1 is an international sport, the majority of the Formula 1 constructors are based in the United Kingdom.

Harrius Potter et Philosophi Lapis

An academic Peter Needham has translated several of the Harry Potter novels into Latin.

Harry Potter and the Standby Dentists

The producers of the Harry Potter movies had dentists on standby during filming. Due to the young age of the cast many lost their first teeth during filming and being able to give them fake teeth quickly ensured there were no continuity errors and that no time was lost reshooting.

Shortest telegram

The shortest telegram exchange in the English language was between writer Oscar Wilde and his publisher. He was living in Paris at the time and he telegrammed his publisher in Britain to see how his new book was doing. The exchange went as follows:

Wilde: ?
The publisher: !

SMS

The first SMS was "Merry Christmas".

Silent or Stealth SMS messages are used to locate a person's whereabouts. They do not show up on the screen of the phone or trigger any acoustical signal when received. Their usual purpose is that the mobile provider can, at the behest of the police, capture data such as the subscriber identifier (IMSI) or the user's location.

The 140-character limit on Tweets is related to the 160-character limit on SMS, 20 characters are reserved for the username + 140 for the tweet text.

Oil Fund

Norway has the world's largest sovereign wealth fund and it is commonly referred to simply as The Oil Fund (Norwegian: Oljefondet). It is estimated to hold one percent of global equity markets.

Tactical Nuclear Penguin

Tactical Nuclear Penguin is a beer brewed by BrewDog in Scotland and it contains 32% alcohol. It uses the Eisbock process to reach these levels of alcohol. This process makes use of the fact that as water freezes at a higher temperature than alcohol, by cooling the beer to the freezing point of water the ice can be removed leaving a more a beer with a higher alcohol content.

BrewDog also make a 41% beer called Sink the Bismarck.

Brewing ultra high alcohol beers > 50% is a very modern phenomenon with many brewers competing for bragging rights. These are generally made in extremely limited production runs.

<u>Harvard Business School</u>

Harvard Business School refused entrance to Warren Buffett who went on to become the world's most successful investor.

<u>Harvard alumna</u>

Film star Natalie Portman attended Harvard where she completed a bachelor's degree in psychology.

<u>Wine bottle sizes</u>

Split	¼ standard bottle
Half	1/2 standard bottle
Bottle	standard bottle
Magnum	2 standard bottles
Jeroboam	4 or 6 standard bottles
Methuselah	8 standard bottles
Salmanazar	12 standard bottles
Balthazar	16 standard bottles
Nebuchadnezzar	20 standard bottles

<u>Guinness</u>

Guinness was first brewed in County Kildare not in Dublin.

A mixture of 75% nitrogen and 25% carbon dioxide is used to dispense it.

Guinness was one of the first trademarked products in Ireland, with the distinctive harp being trademarked shortly after the passing of the Trade Marks Registration Act of 1875.

Guinness is not the only stout sold in Ireland: Heineken brew both Murphy's and Beamish stout in Cork and smaller craft brewers produce stouts at locations dotted around the country.

The Guinness harp has the straight edge to the left whereas the Irish National symbol has the straight edge to the right.

Dracula

Dracula was written by an Irish novelist Abraham "Bram" Stoker, and several aspects from the book draw inspiration from places and occurrences around Dublin.

Dogdays

In 2007, the United States Federal Drug Administration approved Prozac, an antidepressant commonly prescribed to humans, for the purpose of treating "canine separation anxiety." Eli Lilly currently sells it for dogs and other animals under the brand name Reconcile.

Uncompromising

There is no specific word for compromise in Arabic, Turkish or Farsi.

Victorian Postal Service

In London during the Victorian era, many postal districts had 12 deliveries a day.

Hyena poo

Hyena faeces are a chalky white due to the calcium from the bones of the animals they consume as part of their diet.

Infinite loop

The reason "switching it off and on again" fixes many computer problems is that computer programs are written as loops, and restarting the program removes it from the area with the problem. It also explains why many issues recur at exactly the same place over and over again!

Spit on his brother

According to Orthodox Judaism, if a couple has no kids and the husband dies, the widow must marry his younger brother. If she wishes to marry someone else, they first must perform a ceremony prescribed in Deuteronomy 25:5: the widow should approach the younger brother, take off his shoes and spit in his face.

Lock, stock and barrel

The expression lock, stock and barrel came from the way guns were purchased: as they were expensive, they were typically purchased in those three constituent parts.

Sonic boom

The crack sound a whip makes is produced when a section of the whip moves faster than the speed of sound, creating a small sonic boom.

Coffee shops

London's first coffeehouse was opened by a Greek named Pasqua Roseé in 1652 who had developed a taste for coffee while working in Turkey. He wanted to replicate the coffee concept in London and opened his coffeehouse there. The venture proved so successful that many more sprung up. These coffee houses fulfilled both social and business needs and they were the social media equivalent of their day. News and ideas were exchanged, opinions were debated and coffee shops became hotbeds of political discussion. Some of these coffee houses even led to the creation of businesses such as Lloyd's insurance.

Lloyd's insurance

Edward Lloyd opened a coffee house in 1688 in Tower Street, London. The unique selling point of Lloyd's Coffee House was that he reserved a table for ship's captains in his coffee house and this, along with the provision of reliable shipping news in his establishment, meant that it became popular with sailors, merchants, and ship-owners.

Wealthy individuals who frequented Lloyd's coffee house started syndicates where they would share the risk of insuring ships and their cargoes. These syndicate members would sign their names one under the other on the policy and hence become known as "underwriters".

In 1691 Lloyd's moved his coffee house to Lombard Street and though he was not personally involved in insurance, his coffee shop remained the centre for marine insurance so the business moved with him. In 1769 again Lloyd moved his coffee shop moved to Pope's Head Alley as New Lloyd's Coffee House and in 1771, seventy-nine underwriters who did business at Lloyd's coffee shop subscribed £100 each and Lloyd's Coffee House became The Society of Lloyd's of London and it was incorporated in 1871.

Lloyd's current home on Lime Street is a Grade I listed building as of 2011; it was the youngest structure ever to obtain this status just 25 years after it was built.

Liger

A liger is the offspring of a male lion and a female tiger; it is the largest of all known living cats. Fully grown ligers can weigh over 400 kg. A tiglon on the other hand is the offspring of a male tiger and a female lion. Even rarer still is a litigon, the offspring of a male lion and a female tigon.

Dream inspiration

There are many instances in history where dreams have furthered scientific understanding or discovery. Some examples include:

The German chemist **Friedrich** August Kekulé discovered the ring shape of the benzene molecule after daydreaming a snake seizing its own tail.

Elias Howe, the inventor of the sewing machine, struggled initially to make it work. His first attempt, using a needle that was pointed at both ends with an eye in the middle was a failure. Then one night he dreamt he was taken prisoner by a group of natives who danced around him with spears. He noticed that their spears all had holes near their tips. His dream inspired him to locate a hole at the tip of the needle and this made his invention successful.

Ill-chosen website names

Two of the more unsuccessful website names were therapistfinder and teacherstalking, the component words are fine on their own but don't work well when run together.

Unsuccessful product names

Chevy Nova - Nova means "no go" in Spanish which isn't a connotation one wants associated with a car.

Irish Mist – An Irish Cream Liqueur didn't do so well in the German market where mist means manure

Mitsubishi Pajero - This had to be renamed for the Spanish market as pajero translates as he who fiddles with himself for sexual gratification in Spanish.

Gin

Is vodka flavoured with juniper berries.

Cocktail cure

In the eighteenth-century malaria was a persistent problem in India and other tropical regions. It was discovered that quinine could be used to prevent the disease. Quinine had a bitter, unpleasant taste so British officers in India took to adding a mixture of water, sugar, lime and gin to the quinine in order to make the drink more palatable hence the name gin and tonic.

First actual computer bug

On the 9th September 1947 the Harvard University Mark II Aiken Relay Calculator (an early computer) began to exhibit some problems and a subsequent investigation showed that there was a moth trapped between the points of Relay number 70, in Panel F. The computers operators removed the moth and affixed it to the log, which reads as "First actual case of bug being found."

Umami

Umami is a Japanese word used to describe a certain type of savoury taste and is one of the five basic tastes (together with sweet, sour, bitter and salty). People taste umami via receptors for glutamate. Glutamate is commonly found in its salt form as the food additive monosodium glutamate (MSG). Parmesan cheese has very high levels of naturally occurring glutamate so is very high on the umami scale.

Antarctica versus Arctic

Arctic comes from the Greek arktikos meaning northern from the Greek arktos meaning bear.

Antarctica means opposite of Arctic.

Antarctica is the only continent without a time zone. The communities of scientists in Antarctica tend to keep either the time relating to their native land or the supply lines that bring them food and other essential goods. One can walk all the 24 time zones in a few seconds.

Antarctica is home to the penguin, the Arctic home to the polar bear. The only place you will see both together is the zoo.

Antarctica is the only continent where pumpkins can't be grown.

ATMs

The first ATM or Automated Teller Machine was opened at Barclays Bank in Enfield Town in North London, United Kingdom, in June 1967.

The world's most southerly ATM is located at the United States McMurdo Antarctic research centre, in Antarctica.

By some estimates there are now over 2 million ATMs installed worldwide.

Of these 95% run Microsoft Windows XP or an earlier version of Microsoft Windows.

Polar bears

A polar bear's fur is translucent rather than white. The longer outer hairs are hollow on the inside and the air trapped inside scatters light and make the bear look white.

Nuclear power

75% of electricity is generated by Nuclear power in France.

Bananas produce small quantities of radiation. This radiation is detectable by Geiger counters.

Living within 50 miles of a coal-fired power station exposes you to more radiation than living within 50 miles of a nuclear power station.

It is possible to visit the site of the Chernobyl disaster, Pripyat. This kind of holiday has been termed extreme tourism.

Rogue Squirrels

Two months after the historic stock market crash in 1987, a stray squirrel gnawing a power cable caused a power failure in Connecticut where the data centre for Nasdaq Stock Exchange is based. This lead to an outage that lasted for over an hour, preventing an estimated 20 million shares from being traded. Sadly, the squirrel met its demise.

New York Stock Exchange

The New York Stock and Exchange Board (the original name of the New York Stock) Exchange came into being on the 17th May 1792 when the Buttonwood Agreement was signed by 24 stockbrokers under a buttonwood tree outside of 68 Wall Street New York. In homage the Economist magazine has a column called Buttonwood.

International Borders

Though we often think of borders between countries as being neat, straight lines or natural features such as rivers etc., the reality is often a little different.
For example, the border of Nepal and China goes through Mount Everest including the peak itself.

The Dutch municipality of Baarle-Nassau shares an unusual border with the Belgian municipality of Baarle-Hertog. Baarle-Hertog consists of 26 separate parcels of land surrounded by Baarle-Nassau, but some parts of Baarle-Hertog also contain areas belonging to Baarle-Nassau. The smallest part belonging to Belgium is less than half a hectare with some houses being located in both jurisdictions.

Lying on the border of the Mediterranean Sea and the Atlantic Ocean is Ceuta an autonomous Spanish city and exclave located on the north coast of North Africa, surrounded by Morocco. The Strait of Gibraltar separates Ceuta from the Iberian Peninsula.

Morocco asserts a claim over Ceuta while facing Ceuta across the of Strait of Gibraltar is Gibraltar, a British Overseas Territory, which the Spanish government asserts a claim over!

<u>Tank you</u>

If a military tank on display has its gun pointing downwards, it means it's a captured one (belonging to the enemy).

If the tank on display has its gun pointing upwards, it means it's a decommissioned one (belonging to the country where it's displayed).

<u>Saccharin</u>

Saccharin was first produced in 1878 by Constantin Fahlberg, a chemist experimenting on coal tar derivatives in Ira Remsen's laboratory at the Johns Hopkins University. While working on these compounds, which were extracted from coal tar, he noticed a sweet taste from his hands. This sweet taste was due to the compound that we now know as saccharin.

Saccharin is approximately 300 times as sweet as sucrose or table sugar.

<u>Playing cards</u>

Playing cards were invented in imperial China as early as the 9th century.

The king of hearts is the only one of the kings on a deck of cards that doesn't have a moustache.

<u>E numbers</u>

E numbers are codes for chemicals that are permitted for use as food additives within the European Union and Switzerland (the "E" stands for "Europe").

They are displayed on food labels throughout the European Union and Switzerland. The safety assessment and approval of these food additives are the responsibility of the European Food Safety Authority.

The are classified in the following ranges:

E100–E199 (colours)
E200–E299 (preservatives)
E300–E399 (antioxidants, acidity regulators)
E400–E499 (thickeners, stabilizers, emulsifiers)
E500–E599 (acidity regulators, anti-caking agents)
E600–E699 (flavour enhancers)
E700–E799 (antibiotics)
E900–E999 (glazing agents and sweeteners)
E1000–E1599 (additional chemicals)

E120 Cochineal is made from bugs, and unappealing as this may seem other synthetic red dyes are derived from either coal or petroleum by-products which may carry health risks.

Sylvester Stallone

Sylvester Stallone wrote the screenplay for Rocky in 20 hours. He received an Oscar nomination for Best Original Screenplay.

Alka Seltzer

Alka Seltzer massively increased their sales by switching to recommending two tablets on their packaging and depicting two tablets dropping into a glass of water in every commercial. This was further reinforced by the creation of the "plop plop fizz fizz" jingle.

A similar dramatic increase in sales of shampoo was attributed to the "Lather. Rinse. Repeat." instruction.

Buffalo times eight

Buffalo buffalo Buffalo buffalo buffalo buffalo Buffalo buffalo" is a grammatically correct sentence in American English.

For the meaning to make sense it helps to know that there is an American city called Buffalo in New York State and that American English has a verb "to buffalo" which means to bully or intimidate.

FedEx funding

There is a – possibly apocryphal - story that logistics company FedEx had only $5000 in its bank account and faced a $24,000 aviation fuel bill. Founder Fred Smith was allegedly turned down for a loan by General Dynamics so Smith took the $5,000 and flew to Las Vegas. In Las Vegas he played blackjack and won $27,000 which was enough to meet the fuel bill and allowed for the operation to continue.

The FedEx logo has an arrow going from left to right between the E and the X but in Arabic this is reversed as Arabic is read from right to left.

Public transport conspiracy

In 1936 a consortium of American companies (including General Motors, Firestone Tire, Standard Oil, and Phillips Petroleum) with vested interest in the success of the automobile industry collaborated to establish three front companies called National City Lines, Pacific City Lines, and American City Lines.

The strategic goal of these front companies was to acquire local transit systems throughout the country, which at the time were primarily streetcar and light-rail lines, tear them up, convert them to bus operations, and encourage further American dependency on the automobile.

The Manhattan Solstice

Exactly twice a year the setting sun in Manhattan New York aligns perfectly with the east-west streets, creating a luminescent orange flare that lights up the city's streets.

So if you were standing on any of the city's streets looking west you would see the sun setting directly opposite at the other end of the street.

Odd place names

Hell is a place in Norway. Hell used to be served by a daily flight AY666 from Copenhagen. Fittingly the last flight was on Friday 13th 2017.

The Scottish hamlet of Dull is twinned with the community of Boring, Oregon.

Low background steel

Low background steel is steel that was produced before the first atmospheric nuclear explosions in 1945. These and later atmospheric tests raised the level of radioactive dust and hence radiation in the atmosphere. For most uses this low level of radioactivity is not an issue. However, for certain specialist uses such as sensors like Geiger counters, it is preferable to use materials that are not as radioactive such as low background steel.

Concorde

The iconic Concorde's take-off speed was 320 km/h.

It was the first aircraft to have computer controlled engine air intakes: these slowed the air down from 1600 km/h in a space of approximately 5 metres.

Concorde holds the world record for the fastest commercial transatlantic crossing in just 2 hours, 54 minutes and 45 seconds from New York's John F. Kennedy airport to London's Heathrow airport.

After the fatal Paris crash, Concorde's fuel tanks were strengthened with a bulletproof Kevlar lining.

Black boxes

Aircraft flight data recorder or black boxes are in fact generally coloured bright orange to make them easier to find. They are usually mounted in the aircraft's empennage (tail section), where they are more likely to survive a severe crash.

Longer days

NASA calculated that China's Three Gorges dam increases the length of the day about 0.06 microseconds. The effect is observed due to an increase in moment of inertia by raising 39 trillion kilograms of water 175 meters above the sea level.

Apple

Steve Jobs' employee number was 0, Steve Wozniak was employee number 1 and Jobs did not want to be number 2.

The iconic 1984 ad for Macintosh was directed by Ridley Scott who went on to direct Alien.

59 secs in a minute

The punctuality of the Swiss train system is world famous and one of the aids to achieving the legendary accuracy is that the clocks in Swiss train stations only take 59 seconds instead of 60 to complete a revolution of the clock (i.e. 1 minute). The second hand then waits 2 seconds at the 12 o'clock position for a signal from the central timekeeping servers to start the next minute.

First past 100mph

The Flying Scotsman was the first train to exceed 100 miles per hour (160.9 kilometres per hour), more remarkable was that it was a steam train and that this speed often isn't bettered by today's trains almost 80 years later.

Canary Islands

The Canary Islands are named after puppies: their Latin name is insularia canaria meaning islands of the puppies.

Caffeinated

One grande-size of Starbucks' coffee contains 320 mg caffeine, which is 4 times more than in a regular can of Red Bull.

Smoking

Nicotine was named after the tobacco plant, which was in turn named after a Frenchman Jean Nicot, who introduced the tobacco plant to France in 1560.

Helipads

The H on a helipad (helicopter landing pad) is oriented on the axis of the preferred approach and departure path.

Lost and not found

There's a nuclear bomb lost somewhere near Tybee Island off the coast of Georgia, United States of America. In 1958, a Mark-15 2 Megaton nuclear bomb was jettisoned by a B-47 Bomber after it collided with an F-86 fighter plane. It remains missing despite an intensive search.

Facebook blues

The theme for Facebook is mostly blue as its founder Mark Zuckerberg is red green colour blind.

The Facebook message sound contains the notes f,a,c,e.

Mark Zuckerberg's speciality / major was psychology.

The Like button was originally going to be called the Awesome button.

Target

US Retailer Target uses data analytics to predict based on purchases when women become pregnant, so that it can send them coupons and offers to encourage them to shop at Target. Unwittingly, though, they were becoming aware of teenage girls' pregnancy before their parents.

Alphabet

The alphabet is so called because the first two letters in the Greek alphabet were Alpha and beta.

Pangrams

A pangram is a sentence that uses every letter of the alphabet at least once. The best known one is probably "The quick brown fox jumps over the lazy dog." A perfect pangram uses each of the 26 letters just once but they tend to sound a little forced or not make much sense.

Happy birthday

In a set of 23 randomly chosen people, there is a 50% probability of two people having the same birthday. The probability reaches 99% with just 57 people.

For many years Warner/Chappell Music claimed copyright on the song "Happy Birthday to You". In some years they collected upwards of $2 million in royalties.

In 2016 Warner/Chappell paid $14 million to settle a lawsuit challenging its copyright of "Happy Birthday to You." And as a result Happy Birthday is now in the public domain.

LAX

When three-letter airport codes became standard, airports that had been using two letters simply added an X so LA Airport became LAX.

London Underground

The London Underground is also known as the Tube and its stations as

Tube Stations.

There are currently only two Underground station names that contain all five vowels: Mansion House and South Ealing.

There are in the region of 40 disused Underground stations.

The Piccadilly Underground line curves between Knightsbridge and South Kensington stations because it was deemed impossible at the time to drill or dig through the mass of skeletal remains which are buried in Hyde Park.

US TV host Jerry Springer was born in 1944 at Highgate tube station where his mother was sheltering from a German air raid.

There is currently only one Tube station which does not have any letters of the word 'tubular' in it: Epping.

Over half of the London Underground is actually above the ground!

Piggy Banks

The name for piggy banks comes from the use of family money jars in the Middle Ages made from a type of clay called pygg.

Strongest

The tongue is considered to be the body's strongest muscle and is also the only one not connected at both ends.

Jam versus marmalade

Jam and marmalade differ in two important ways: their ingredients and the manner in which they are prepared. Both spreads are made with whole fruit, sugar and water, but only marmalade is prepared with a fruit's peels. Because of the importance of peels, marmalades are made almost exclusively from citrus fruits, while jams can be made from almost any fruits and vegetables.

Tomato ketchup versus tomato sauce

The difference between tomato ketchup and tomato sauce is that tomato sauce has added herbs and spices.

Hot hot hot

Chilli peppers have their own scale called the Scoville scale to measure their spiciness. The scale is named after its creator Wilbur Scoville. The scale indicates the amount of capsaicin present per unit of dry mass.

The chemical component that makes chillies spicy is also the one used in pepper sprays, which are used to repel bears and by law enforcement agencies.

Biscuit versus cakes

When biscuits get stale they get softer and when cakes get stale they get harder.

The philosophical question of whether a Jaffa Cake was a cake or biscuit arose in the United Kingdom. The significance of the borderline between cakes and biscuits is that a cake is zero-rated for value add tax in the event that it is covered in chocolate, whereas a biscuit is standard-rated if wholly or partly covered in chocolate or some product similar in taste and appearance. The court ruled that the Jaffa Cake was indeed a cake.

Golden Screwdriver

Often in the past when a customer ordered the smallest mainframe in a range, IBM shipped a machine with a bigger processor and more memory but with software that prevented the extra processing power or storage being used.

If the customer at a later date wanted an upgraded system an engineer would visit the customer's premises with a "golden screwdriver" and erase the code that was preventing the mainframe from reaching its full potential.

Top tips

A number of factors heavily influence how much restaurant customers tip, these include giving complimentary sweets with the bill, complimenting customers on their menu choice, introducing yourself by name, touching customers, drawing a smiley face on the bill (waitresses only!) and writing "Thank You" on the back of the bill.

The Winklevii

In The Social Network (2010), a film directed by David Fincher about the founding of Facebook, the Winklevii twins are played by actor Armie Hammer. The actor Josh Pence acted as the body double for one twin with Hammer's face superimposed on him.

World's oldest corporation

The Swedish company Stora Kopparberg which started out mining for copper in Falun was granted a charter from King Magnus IV of Sweden in 1347, although the first share in the company (granting the Bishop of Västerås 12.5% ownership) dates from 1288.

Airborne

There are instances while a horse is running when all four hooves are off the ground simultaneously.

Cobblestones

If the stones used in paving are rectangular they are called setts; if they are round they are called cobbles.

Marmite & Guinness

The yeast sludge left over after brewing Guinness is used as one of the main ingredients of the spread Marmite.

Fiendish felines

A cat's miaow has evolved to sound very similar to that of a baby crying.

Venus

Venus spins east to west unlike all the other planets in the solar system, which spin west to east and a day on Venus is longer than its year.

Mining Lifts

The spool for long mining lifts has to be positioned in a certain compass direction in the shaft. The spin of the Earth affects ropes that long and thus could lead to the catastrophic failure of the lift if positioned the wrong way.

Origin of the two fingers salute

It is not, as is often suggested, due to English longbowmen showing their French counterparts that their two fingers remained (legend has it that the French were cutting off two fingers from captured bowmen) as the drawstrings on these longbows would have in fact required three fingers to pull.

Unicorn

The unicorn is the official animal of Scotland. It has been a fixture on the Scottish coat of arms since the 12th century. The current Royal Coat of Arms of the United Kingdom of Great Britain and Northern Ireland still has the English lion on the left and the Scottish unicorn on the right.

Portugal was once ruled from Brazil

Portugal was once ruled from Brazil when John VI of Portugal was forced to flee there when Napoleon's troops invaded Portugal.

Panama hats

Panama hats are made in Ecuador.

John Logie Baird

John Logie Baird was a pioneering Scottish inventor in the field of television. Though the development of television was as the result of the work of many, John Logie Baird was a key contributor.

Baird transmitted the first television picture in greyscale on the 2nd October 1925, the world's first colour transmission on 3 July 1928 and the world's first colour broadcast on the 4th February 1938. The latter involved sending a mechanically scanned 120-line image from Baird's Crystal Palace studios to a projection screen at London's Dominion Theatre.

In Australia the annual television awards are known as the "Logies" in his honour.

Phonovision was a proof-of-concept format developed in the late 1920s by Baird for recording a mechanical television signal on phonograph records. Recently it has become possible to decode some of these early recordings.

Pakistan is an acronym

The name was developed by a group of students at Cambridge University who issued a pamphlet in 1933 called "Now or Never".

"Now or Never" used letters from the names of the five northern regions of the British Raj: The initial letters from Punjab, Afghania Province (North-West Frontier Province), Kashmir, Sindh, and the tan from Baluchistan with the letter i added to ease pronunciation.

Though Pakistan was conceived in 1947 as an independent homeland for Indian Muslims, India now has a larger Muslim population than Pakistan.

Eiffel Tower

Images of the Eiffel tower by day are not copyrighted but the light show at night is copyrighted.

The heat of the sun makes the tower expand by up to 15 centimetres.

Originally it took 60 tonnes of paint to paint the tower. It is now repainted every seven years.

During World War 2, a Mustang P-51 pilot William Overstreet Jr. flew underneath the Eiffel Tower's arches. He was in pursuit of a German fighter plane, which he ultimately shot down.

No fingerprints

The anti-cancer medication capecitabine is an orally administered chemotherapeutic agent used in the treatment of metastatic breast and colorectal cancers one of whose side effects is that the patient may experience the loss of their fingerprints.

200-billion-dollar mistake

Berkshire Hathaway, the investment vehicle of the world's most successful investor Warren Buffett, is named after what he considers to be his biggest mistake an unprofitable textile mill.

Broke the Bank of England

George Soros famously broke the Bank of England when his Quantum Fund shorted the pound sterling to the value of over £10 billion; the UK were forced to withdraw from the European Exchange Rate Mechanism and devalue the pound and Soros profited to the tune of over $1 billion.

In a jiffy

As well as being an expression a jiffy has now become a measurement of a specified period of time. The length of time depends on the particular application. In electronics, a jiffy is the time between alternating current power cycles (1/50 or 1/60 of a second in most mains power supplies). Whereas in physics it's the time it takes for light to travel one fermi (approximately the size of a nucleon).

Tittle

The dot on top of the letter 'i' and 'j' is known as a tittle.

King Bluetooth

The wireless technology Bluetooth is named after King Harald Bluetooth who united Scandinavia into a single kingdom. The logo is his initials HB written in old Nordic runes.

Handy

The fuel gauge in cars often includes a small arrow that indicates the side of the fuel tank door. When there is no arrow the side with the filler hose should indicate the side for the fuel tank door (i.e. hose on left, fuel tank door on left)

Seinfeld

Kramer did not appear in two episodes of Seinfeld. The first was "The Pen" in the second season and the second was "The Chinese Restaurant" in the third season, in which Jerry, Elaine and George wait to be seated at a Chinese restaurant. The actor Michael Richards was so upset about being omitted that they never made another episode where all 4 stars did not appear.

Nein!

BMW was forced to recall a female-voiced navigation system on its 5 Series cars in the late 1990s after being flooded with calls from German men saying they refused to take directions from a woman.

Mona Lisa

The Mona Lisa was once stolen and the thief got away because they fingerprinted one hand rather than both hands.

The Mona Lisa doesn't have eyebrows. Art historians are not sure whether they were never there or got removed in an over zealous cleaning attempt.

Flavour graveyard

Ben and Jerry's, the ice cream makers, have a flavour graveyard where discontinued flavours get a head stone and an epitaph.

Weapons of mass destruction

Many sources point to a 1937 address by the then Archbishop of Canterbury, Cosmo Gordon Lang, as the first time the phrase "weapons of mass destruction" was used. In a report at the time, London's Times newspaper quoted Lang as referring to wars in China and Spain and saying: "Who can think without horror of what another widespread war would mean, waged as it would be with all the new weapons of mass destruction."

Pencil versus Pen

An apocryphal story details that for the Apollo space program, NASA spent a million dollars developing a special pen that could write upside down and that the Russian's used a simpler solution namely a pencil. However, after the fatal Apollo 1 fire NASA switched from using flammable materials in the pure oxygen capsule environment as a safety measure.

Vowels in correct order

These words have all the vowels in the correct order: abstemious meaning restrained with regard to eating and drinking, and facetious meaning in jest.

Unilever

One company Unilever buys 6% of the world's tomatoes and 5% of the worlds onions, mostly for their range of Knorr soups and Ragu pasta sauces.

Unilever is also the world's largest manufacturer of ice cream and includes the Ben and Jerry's, Algida, Walls and Magnum brands.

Unilever came about as an unlikely alliance between a soap and a margarine company; the common ground was that palm oil was an ingredient used in the manufacture of both products.

Flag Facts

The flag of Paraguay is the only flag in the world that's different in the front and in the back.

The flag of Denmark, "Dannebrog," is the oldest state flag in the world still in use by an independent nation. It was adopted in 1219.

Nepal's flag is the world's only non-quadrilateral national flag

The Mozambique flag includes an image of an AK-47 assault rifle

Aardvark

The aardvark is a medium-sized, burrowing, nocturnal mammal native to Africa. It is the only living species of the order Tubulidentata, although other prehistoric species and genera of Tubulidentata are known.

Beer after exercise

Some studies suggest that beer after exercise is a better aid to rehydration than water.

Woodpecker

A woodpecker's head experiences decelerations of 1200g as it drums on a tree at up to 22 times per second so it has a complex shock absorber to protect its brain from the massive forces it experiences.

Not Obelus

The sign for the division operation in mathematics is called Obelus.

Elementary

Sherlock Holmes never uttered the words "Elementary my dear Watson"; he said both "elementary" and "my dear Watson" just not both together.

Chip art

Chip art refers to microscopic artwork built into integrated circuits, also called chips. Prior to 1984, these doodles also served a practical purpose. If a competitor produced a similar chip, and examination showed it contained the same doodles, then this was strong evidence that the design was copied and not independently derived.

College dropouts

Bill Gates dropped out of Harvard to create Microsoft, Mark Zuckerberg dropped out of Harvard to create Facebook, Steve Jobs dropped out of Reed College to start Apple and Michael Dell dropped out of University of Texas to start Dell.

Oracle

The Oracle relational database product, which powers most of the world's largest websites grew out of a CIA project that Oracle founder Larry Ellison worked on. The name Oracle was the codename of that CIA funded project.

Fears

Coulrophobia – fear of clowns

Friggatriskaidekaphobia - fear of Friday the 13th
Omphalophobia – fear of bellybuttons

<u>United States ZIP codes</u>

ZIP, an acronym for Zone Improvement Plan, is properly written in capital letters and was chosen to suggest that the mail travels more efficiently, and therefore more quickly, when senders use the code in the postal address. It was an innovation of a US Postal Service employee.

10118 is assigned to the Empire State building.

12345 is assigned to the world headquarters for General Electric in Schenectady,
New York.

20252 is assigned to Smokey Bear, mascot of the U.S. Forest Service.

32976 is assigned to a mobile home park at Barefoot Bay, Brevard County, Florida.

48222 is assigned to a marine post office in Detroit, Michigan used to route mail to and from passing Great Lakes commercial vessels, the last of its kind in the ZIP code system.

77230 was assigned in 2005 for mail delivery to victims of Hurricane Katrina
being housed at the Houston Astrodome, it still operates as a PO box.

89412 is assigned to the Burning Man festival, Blackrock city, Nevada

<u>United Kingdom Postal codes:</u>

There are a number of special postcodes in the United Kingdom such as for
letters to Father Christmas (SAN TA1)
Egg banking (DE99 3GG)

Royal Mail headquarters (EC4Y 0HQ)

Directorship

Bill Gates holds only one directorship other than Microsoft: it is at Berkshire Hathaway and he gets paid only a few thousand dollars per annum.

Yahoo

Yahoo stands for Yet Another Hierarchical Officious Oracle

At one stage Yahoo had the opportunity to buy Google for $1,000,000.

Ocean versus sea

Oceans are vast bodies of water that cover roughly 70% of the earth. Seas are smaller and partially enclosed by land. The five oceans of the earth are in reality one large interconnected water body. In contrast, there are over 50 smaller seas scattered around the world.

Nuclear reactor

London once had a small nuclear reactor operating in Greenwich hospital. It was installed in 1962 for training purposes as the Royal Naval Staff College was located there.

Continent hopping

At times it's possible to walk from America (Alaska) to Russia, across the Bering Strait. Although if you do so you will almost certainly get arrested by Russian border guards if you haven't sought permission in advance.

Tom Crean

Tom Crean was an Irish seaman and Antarctic explorer. He was a participant in of three of the four major British expeditions to Antarctica.

During the ill fated Terra Nova Expedition, Crean's 56-kilometre solo walk across the Ross Ice Shelf to save the life of Edward Evans led to him receiving the Albert Medal.

Crean's third and final Antarctic adventure was the Imperial Trans-Antarctic Expedition on the Endurance led by Ernest Shackleton, in which he served as second officer.

Crean's contributions to these expeditions sealed his reputation as both a tough and dependable polar traveller, and earned him a total of three Polar medals.

After the Endurance expedition he returned to the Royal Navy, and when he retired from his naval career in 1920 he moved back to his home town of Annascaul, County Kerry, Ireland where he and his wife Ellen opened a public house called the "South Pole Inn". He lived there quietly and unobtrusively until his death in 1938.

Blackbird SR-71

The Lockheed SR-71 Blackbird was developed as an ultra high-speed reconnaissance aircraft during the Cold War. It was developed as a response to the downing of Francis Gary Power's U-2 in 1960 by a Russian Surface to Air missile. The U-2 was slow and vulnerable to missile attack and aircraft interception, the Blackbird was designed so that it could outrun missiles launched against it and aircraft sent to intercept it.

In 1974 a Blackbird flew from New York to London in a record 1 hour 54 minutes and 56.4 seconds a record that still stands. This is approximately an hour faster than Concorde's record.

The Blackbird burns conventional JP-7 jet fuel, which is difficult to ignite, so to start the engines, triethylborane (TEB), which ignites on contact with air, was injected to ignite the JP-7. The TEB produced a characteristic green flame that could often be seen during engine ignition.

Much like astronauts, pilots of the Blackbird had to wear spacesuits and the favoured meal was the low residue steak and eggs popular with astronauts.

A replacement for the SR-71 Blackbird has been proposed. This replacement, designated the SR-72, would be capable of cruising at hypersonic speeds of up to Mach 6.

<u>Pepsi Challenge</u>

John Sculley was a senior vice president of sales and marketing at Pepsi when he conceived of the Pepsi Challenge.

This was a novel advertising campaign that claimed that Pepsi Cola tasted better than Coca Cola using heavily advertised comparative taste tests.

The Pepsi Challenge television ads featured lifelong Coca Cola drinkers participating in blind taste tests with Pepsi Cola. In the ads Pepsi Cola was always chosen as the favourite by the participants.

Interestingly Sculley himself took the taste test and picked Coke instead of Pepsi!

John Sculley went on to be CEO of Apple and famously fired Steve Jobs.

<u>555 numbers</u>

Telephone numbers with the prefix 555 are widely used for fictitious telephone numbers in North American television shows, films, video games, and other media.

During the 1960s phone companies began encouraging the producers of television shows and movies to use the 555 prefix for fictional telephone numbers.

In an in-joke, 555 numbers are mentioned in the 1993 action film The Last Action Hero, starring Arnold Schwarzenegger. The character of Danny Madigan tries to convince Schwarzenegger's character that he is inside a movie by pointing out that 555 numbers give at most 9,999 possible telephone numbers, Schwarzenegger's character replies that area codes would solve that problem and O'Brien's character drops the subject.

Who are you going to call!? Ghostbusters!?

Well then you should know their number 555-2368 (2368 is CENT spelt out on a phone and is short for central).

In the tv comedy Seinfeld, Kramer's phone number is 555-FILK - In one episode Kramer's keeps getting calls intended for Moviefone -- which is 555-FILM.

Henry Ford Museum

The Henry Ford Museum complex in Dearborn, Michigan consists of a 9-acre museum building and an 80-acre outdoor complex.

The museum building is home to such exhibits as the actual Rosa Park bus and the 600 tonne Allegheny locomotive.

One can ride around the outdoor park in a restored orginal Model T car.

George Boole

Boole was an English mathematician, philosopher and logician. He worked in the fields of differential equations and algebraic logic. As the inventor of the prototype of what is now called Boolean logic, which became the basis of the modern digital computer, he is now regarded as a key figure in the foundation of the field of computer science.

Four Wheel Drive

The Jensen FF was a four-wheel drive Grand Tourer car produced by the British manufacturer Jensen Motors between 1966 and 1971. It was the first non all-terrain production car equipped with four-wheel drive and an anti-lock braking system. It predated the use of four-wheel drive by both Audi and Subaru.

Fossilised Lightning

Fossilised lightning is called a Fulgurite (from the Latin fulgur meaning thunderbolt) and is natural hollow glass tube formed in quartzose sand, silica, or soil by lightning strikes.

They are formed when lightning melts silica on a conductive surface and fuses the grains together; the fulgurite tube is the cooled product.

This process occurs in less than a second, and leaves evidence of the lightning's path.

747 Jigsaw

A Boeing 747-400 Jumbo jet has six million parts approximately half of which are fasteners.

Vavoy

Dr. d'Armond Speers, an American computational linguist, raised his son Alec to speak Klingon as a first language up to the age of 5. His son did not enjoy it and this lead to the projects abandonment!

Phytophthora infestans

Phytophthora infestans is an oomycete that causes the serious potato disease known as potato blight. The effects of potato blight in Ireland from 1845 – 57 were one of the factors which caused over one million to starve to death and forced another two million to emigrate. Many of these emigrants moved to the United States, which is why now it is estimated that over 40 million Americans claim that they are of Irish extraction.

Halloween pumpkins

The tradition of carving pumpkins at Halloween was initiated by Irish immigrants in America who had carved turnips in their homeland to celebrate All Hallows Eve or Halloween festival from their country of origin. In Ireland they had carved turnips but the readily available and more easily carved pumpkin in America soon took over and a tradition was born.

The knowledge

London black cab taxi drivers have to pass a test called the Knowledge. It includes the major arterial routes throughout London and 25,000 streets within a 10 kilometre radius of Charing Cross. This course is so intensive that it effects a change in the hippocampus, the part of the brain that deals with spatial awareness and memory.

Cornish Pasty

Cornish pasties were popularised by Cornish miners. The side-crimped pasties allowed the miner to eat the pasty holding the thick edge which could then be discarded. Eating the pasty in this manner ensured that dirt or contaminants from mining were not transferred from the miner's fingers to his food or mouth.

In 2011 "Cornish pasty" was awarded Protected Geographical Indication status by the European Commission.

Shepherd's pie

Shepherd's pie is not made of shepherds but instead their charges, lambs! The beef equivalent is cottage pie and the vegetarian equivalent garden pie. It was a way of using up scraps of meat and assorted vegetables.

Amusement parks

Dyrehavsbakken located 10 km to the north of Copenhagen is the world's oldest amusement park still in operation.

Its first opened in the late 16th century and the entertainers and artists who performed here attracted crowds from all over Europe.

Cabarets were added in 1866, and the first wooden roller coaster was introduced in 1932.

Rubbish/trash/waste

Rubbish is the English word for waste that is thrown away. Garbage and trash are the American English terms for wet and dry waste respectively that is thrown away. Litter is waste left in streets and other public places.

Tuxedo

The correct name for a tuxedo is a dinner jacket. Its name comes from its popularity in Tuxedo Park area of Hudson Valley, New York's stomping ground for the socially elite.

Nikola Tesla

Nikola Tesla was a Croatian born inventor, electrical engineer, mechanical engineer and physicist, who played a part in the discovery of a huge number of modern innovations that we take for granted.

He studied and worked in Europe before moving to America where he began working for Thomas Edison. He and Edison fundamentally disagreed as to whether electricity should be transported via direct current or the alternating current electrical system that Tesla invented. Ultimately the alternating current electrical system became the global standard.

As a result of a campaign by the Oatmeal.com, Tesla's former laboratory was purchased as a result of an Indiegogo project and work has begun on restoring it as a museum in his honour.

Telsa the car company is named in his honour as a pioneer in the field of electricity.

Alaska

On 30th March 1867, on the instructions of Secretary of State William H. Seward, America purchased Alaska from Russia for US$ 7.2 million.

Irish Coffee

In 1943 the original Irish coffee was created by the head chef Joe Sheridan at Foynes' port in the West of Ireland. A Pan America World Airways flying boat had to return due to adverse weather conditions. Sheridan served coffee to which he added whiskey to warm the returning passengers and the Irish Coffee was born.

Seawise Giant

Seawise Giant, later Happy Giant, Jahre Viking, Knock Nevis, Oppama, and finally Mont, was a supertanker and the longest, largest and heaviest ship ever built. Fully laden it displaced 657,019 tonnes.

Due to its draft of 24.6 m it could not navigate the English Channel, Suez Canal or Panama Canal.

The Lake Wobegon effect

The Lake Wobegon effect or illusory superiority is a natural human tendency to overestimate one's capabilities relative to your peers. It is named after a fictional town in the U.S. state of Minnesota as depicted in the radio show "A Prairie Home Companion".

The characterisation of the fictional location, where "all the women are strong, all the men are good looking, and all the children are above average," has been used to describe a real and pervasive human tendency to overestimate one's achievements and capabilities in relation to others.

The Lake Wobegon effect, where all or nearly all of a group claim to be above average, has been observed among drivers, CEOs, hedge fund managers, presidents, coaches, radio show hosts, late night comedians, stock market analysts, college students, parents, etc.

Old names for countries

Sri Lanka and Thailand were previously called Ceylon and Siam respectively.

The Czech Republic was previously known as Bohemia, from which we get the word "bohemian", meaning an artist or writer living an unconventional life.

Ireland was previously known by its Latin name, Hibernia.

Zimbabwe was previously known as Rhodesia. It was named after Cecil Rhodes, the founder and managing director of the British South Africa Company, which operated in the area.

Bletchley Park

During the Second World War, Bletchley Park was the site of the United Kingdom's main decryption establishment, the Government Code and Cipher School (GC&CS). Here ciphers and codes of several Axis countries were decrypted, most importantly the ciphers generated by the German Enigma and Lorenz machines.

Cryptanalysts were recruited for excellence in various scientific fields, such as linguistics or mathematics, for possessing the ability to speak many languages or for being an accomplished chess player or even a crossword expert.

In one instance, the ability to solve a Daily Telegraph crossword in under 12 minutes was used as a test. The newspaper was asked to organise a competition, after which each of the successful participants was contacted and asked whether they would be prepared to undertake "a particular type of work as a contribution to the war effort".

QRPFF

QRPFF was a seven-line PERL program that decoded a DRM protected

DVD in real time. It was short enough to be included on t-shirts etc.

<u>Breakfast cereal and computer hacking</u>

Captain Crunch is the nickname of a legendary computer hacker called John Draper. He earned this nickname when he utilised a toy whistle that was given out for free in Cap'n Crunch cereal in the United States in the 1970s to hack the US phone system.

Draper discovered that this toy whistle could emit a tone at precisely 2600 hertz. This exact frequency was used by AT&T to control the operation of it's long distance phone lines.

John Draper used this whistle to learn how to build electronic devices capable of reproducing this 2600 Hz tone and other tones required to control trunk lines.

This resulted in, among other things, the ability to place free phone calls to anywhere in the world and operator like control over the phone system.

To this day the magazine 2600: The Hacker Quarterly is named after this frequency.

<u>Sinister</u>

Sinister comes from the Latin word for left "sinistra".

Autistic people are more likely to be left-handed.

Castles were always built with a spiral staircase that turned clockwise; this was to put the generally right-handed attackers at a disadvantage and give the generally right-handed defenders the advantage.

Athletes have a larger distribution of left-handedness, not because of skill, but due to the fact that the time taken for the brain to send a signal to the left hand is slightly shorter than the time for the brain to send a signal to the right hand (approx. 0.3ms), and as such, the reaction times of left-handed athletes are slightly faster. Interactive sports such as table tennis, badminton, cricket, and tennis have an over-representation of left-handedness, while non-interactive sports such as swimming show no over-representation.

20% more men than women are left-handed.

The boxing stance generally taught to left-handed boxers is the Southpaw stance. Left-handed boxers are often called Southpaws for this reason.

Astronauts

Life insurance for astronauts would have been prohibitively expensive due to the high risks inherent in the space program, so as an alternative the Apollo 11 astronauts signed envelopes and had their friends post them on launch days. These combinations, often called covers, are valuable and in the event of their demise would have become even more so. These covers were addressed to their family and were to provide for them in the case of the astronaut's untimely demise.

Nobel Prize

The Nobel Prize is one of the legacies of Alfred Nobel, whose other main legacy was dynamite.

They are for the most part awarded by Sweden with the exception of the Peace Prize, which is awarded by Norway.

John Paul Sartre was awarded the 1964 Nobel Prize in Literature but turned it down.

Diacritic

A Diacritic or Diacritical Mark are glyphs or marks added to letters to indicate that their pronunciation is different from what might be expected.

Texas

Most of the US is served by just two power grids. However, Texas has its own power grid called the Texas Interconnection, partly because of a historical desire for self-sufficiency and partly because of that famous "Don't Mess with Texas!" attitude.

The state uses more electricity than any other, 44 per cent more than the next largest user California.

Oil prices

Brent and West Texas Intermediate WTI are major trading classifications of sweet light crude oil that serves as a benchmark price for purchases of oil worldwide.

Coffee

Coffee is the second most traded commodity on earth after oil.

Espresso means "forced out" as the coffee is forced out of the beans by high pressured water passing through the grinds.

Cappuccino is so called because of its resemblance to the brown cowls worn by Capuchin monks.

The term Americano comes from American soldiers who during World War 2 ordered espresso diluted with hot water.

Beethoven liked each cup of coffee he drank to be made with exactly 60 coffee beans.

There are two types of coffee plants, Arabica and Robusta.

Arabica has on average about half the caffeine content of Robusta.

In 1675 Charles II, King of England, issued a proclamation banning coffee houses. He stated coffee houses were places where people met to plot against him. He had a point as both the American Revolution and the French Revolution were planned in coffee houses.

The most expensive coffee in the world is Indonesian Kopi Luwak. It is made from beans that are eaten, partly digested and excreted by a small animal the palm civet.

George C. Washington, an English chemist, invented instant coffee in Guatemala in 1906.

Caffeine makes us easier to persuade and that is why car dealerships often have expensive coffee machines as this makes it easier for salespeople to close the deal.

The majority of the coffee we drink today can be traced back to just one tree.

Dunbar number

Dunbar's number is a suggested cognitive limit to the number of people with whom one can maintain stable social relationships.

Dunbar carried out surveys of villages and tribes and their sizes also appeared to approximate to this predicted value. This including 150 as the estimated size of a Neolithic farming village; 150 as the splitting point of Hutterite settlements; 200 as the upper bound on the number of academics in a discipline's sub-specialization; 150 as the basic unit size of professional armies in Roman antiquity and in modern times since the 16th century; and notions of appropriate company size.

The average number of friends a user has on Facebook is around this number (with allowances for a few people added in haste that one feels unable to defriend!)

PARC the Palo Alto Research Center had an upper limit of 150 people for this reason.

Military and drugs

Many recreational drugs trace their origin or popularisation to former military uses.

Methamphetamine was used by both Allied and Axis forces during World War II.

The German company Temmler produced methamphetamine under the trademark Pervitin to supply the German armed Forces It was thought to attenuate anxiety and increase performance and concentration.

The Japanese brand of methamphetamine called Philopon/Hiropon was widely distributed to factory workers, soldiers and kamikaze pilots. The drug contributed heavily to the Japanese attitude of never surrendering, and especially in the willingness of kamikaze pilots to follow through with their suicide missions.

After rain smell

Often after it rains there is a characteristic smell, this smell is caused by bacteria called Actinomycetes which grow in soil when conditions are damp and warm. When the soil dries out, the bacteria produces spores in the soil, the wetness and force of the raindrops kick these tiny spores up into the air giving that characteristic just rained smell.

Kit Kat

The idea for the Kit Kat bar originated from a response placed in a suggestion box at the Rowntree factory.

Kit Kat was originally known as Rowntree's Chocolate Crisp.

After World War II due to milk shortages Kit Kat was made from dark chocolate and the wrapper was blue, not red.

In 1958, Donald Gilles, an advertising executive at JWT Orland, created the iconic advertising line "Have a Break, Have a Kit Kat".

A three-finger Kit Kat is produced for the Middle East to match a denomination of the local currency, making the product a convenient, one-coin purchase

Kit Kat made the 1997 Guinness Book of World Records by selling 13.2 billion Kit Kats worldwide in 1995

London Underground mosquito

A new species of mosquito evolved on the London Underground system. This sub-species of mosquito, Culex pipiens molestus by biologists, broke off from the above-ground population of Culex pipiens pipiens mosquitoes in the mid-19th Century when the London Underground was constructed. This new species adjusted to the warmer conditions underground.

Originally the above ground mosquitoes fed on birds, which not being available underground meant they had to adapt to alternative food sources, namely the blood of mammals. The recently evolved mosquito preys on mice, rats and occasionally humans. Indeed, during World War II the pest became notorious for attacking Londoners sheltering from the Blitz.

This rapid evolution is highly unusual as changes of this nature usually occurs when species are isolated for thousands rather than tens of years.

Zero-rupee note

A zero-rupee note is issued in India as a means of helping to fight systemic political corruption. The notes are intended for use by citizens to pay government functionaries who solicit bribes in return for services which are supposed to be free.

Zero rupee notes, which are made to resemble the regular 50-rupee banknote of India, are the creation of a non-governmental organisation known as 5th Pillar, they are distributed in different local languages through community and student organisations

On the back of the note is the message "Encourage, Enable and Empower every citizen of India to eliminate corruption at all levels of society" as well as contact information for 5th Pillar and references to the Right to Information act.

Rooftop Racetrack

The Fiat Lingotto Factory built in 1928 unusually featured a rooftop test track. The Matté Trucco design was unusual for a car factory having five floors, with raw materials going in at the ground floor, the cars being built on a line that went up through the building and the finished ones emerging at the test track rooftop level.

This test track also briefly featured in the getaway sequence in the film The Italian Job. The factory became outdated in the 1970s and was finally closed in the 1980s, fortunately though rather than being demolished it was instead converted into a cultural and commercial complex. The test track was retained, and can still be visited today.

High heels

High heels were originally made for men.

Raining diamonds

It regularly rains diamonds on many of the outer planets of our solar system.

Centralia, Pennsylvania

Underneath the city of Centralia, Pennsylvania, a fire has been burning for over 50 years. It started as a small fire in one of the coal mines in 1962 and spread through the mine shafts until it eventually reached an uncontrollable size. The underground heat causes roads and highways to crack open, random cave-ins and emission of poisonous gases including carbon monoxide.

In 1984, the U.S. Congress allocated more than US$42 million to relocate the residents. Most of the residents accepted the buyout offers and moved to the nearby communities of Mount Carmel and Ashland. A few families opted to stay despite warnings from Pennsylvania officials. As a consequence of the fire, the population of the city has decreased from about 1000 people in 1981 to just 10 people in 2010.

Authorities did initially try to extinguish the fire but have for now given up. They do not intend to pursue this issue any further and the current plan is to wait until the fire burns out. It may continue to burn for 250 years.

Al Capone

Despite Al Capone engaging in various criminal activities it was ultimately for tax evasion that he was was tried and convicted of and his incarceration including some time in Alcatraz

Al Capone is credited with the introduction of expiry dates on milk, supposedly a family member became ill after drinking spoilt milk.

Black American Express Card

The American Express Centurion Card, known informally as the Black Card, is an invitation only charge card issued by American Express to platinum card holders after they meet certain criteria, such as spending $250,000 per annum using the card.
Usually the card itself is made of anodised titanium with the information and numbers etched in carbon fibre but in some countries a plastic version of the card is issued, either instead of or in addition to the titanium card.)

Among the perks are the absence of credit limits and a personal concierge service that will source tickets for sold out events and find table reservations at booked out restaurants.

An estimated 17,000 black cards are in circulation worldwide.

The southernmost bar in the world

Vernadsky station, Lat. 65° 15' S, Long. 64° 16' W a former British meteorological base turned Ukrainian science centre in Antarctica is home to the Faraday bar the world's southernmost bar.

The station was established by the British Falkland Islands Dependencies Survey as Base F Winter Island in 1947. The main hut, built on the site of an earlier British Graham Land Expedition hut, was named "Wordie House" after Sir James Wordie, a member of Shackleton's Imperial Trans-Antarctic Expedition who visited during its construction.

This station's most notable contribution to scientific research was the discovery of the hole in the ozone layer. Ukraine took over the operation of the base in February 1996, which was sold by the UK for the symbolic sum of one-pound sterling.

The story behind the building of a bar was that at one stage the station was in need of repair, in particular the pier had become quite rickety. The wood that was delivered to the station to be used for these repairs was instead used by the carpenters to fashion the Antarctic Peninsula's only bar.

Post-it notes

Post-it notes were invented after a weak adhesive was left over from a failed attempt at making super glue.

Cameras on the moon

There are 12 Hasselblad cameras currently sitting on the surface of the moon. The cameras that were used to take those iconic images of the moon's surface between 1969 and 1972 were left there to allow for the 25 kg of lunar rock samples that were brought back instead. Only the film magazines themselves were brought back.

Several different models of Hasselblad cameras were taken into space, all specially modified for the task. The Hasselblad cameras were selected by NASA because of their interchangeable lenses and magazines. Modifications were made to permit ease of use in cramped conditions while wearing spacesuits, such as the replacement of the reflex mirror with an eye-level finder. Modifications by NASA technicians were further refined and incorporated into new models by Hasselblad. For example, development of a 70mm magazine was accelerated to meet the space program.

WD40

WD-40 the lubricant, penetrating oil and water-displacing spray was originally developed to protect Atlas Nuclear missiles from corrosion. The name is an abbreviation for "Water Displacement, 40th formula".

Languages

Portuguese is the seventh most spoken language in the world after English, French, Spanish, Russian, Arabic, Chinese. It has approximately 215 million native speakers and another 25 million non native speakers.

Celtic foster children

Celtic foster children were fostered by the family of the mother as this was a guarantee that they were actually related to them as opposed to the father's side which could be in dispute in the time before DNA testing was available

Illuminati

If you type Illuminati in reverse order into your browser and add .com it will bring you to the United States National Security Agency website.

Apollo 11

The Apollo Guidance Computer used a real time operating system, which enabled astronauts to enter simple commands by typing in pairs of nouns and verbs to control the spacecraft. Electronically it was more basic than a modern day toaster. It had approximately 64 Kbyte of memory and operated at a clockspeed of just 0.043MHz.

Port wine

The world famous fortified wine Port comes from Porto in Portugal. It became very popular in England after the Methuen Treaty of 1703, when merchants were permitted to import it with a low level of duty, while simultaneously war with France deprived English wine drinkers of French wine.

The long trip to England often resulted in spoiled wine so fortification of the wine was introduced to improve the shipping and shelf life of the wine for its journey.

Monty Hall problem

The Monty Hall problem is a probability puzzle loosely based on the American television game show Let's Make a Deal and named after the show's original host, Monty Hall.

It became famous in the following form, as a question from a reader's letter quoted in Marilyn vos Savant's "Ask Marilyn" column in Parade magazine in 1990

Suppose you're on a game show, and you're given the choice of three doors: Behind one door is a car; behind the others, goats. You pick a door, say No. 1, and the host, who knows what's behind the doors, opens another door, say No. 3, which has a goat. He then says to you, "Do you want to pick door No. 2?" Is it to your advantage to switch your choice?

Mathematically the answer is that you should swap and that doing so gives you a 2/3 chance of winning the car. A simple explanation is that players initially have a 2/3 chance of picking a goat and those who swap always get the opposite of their original choice. So players who always swap have a 2/3 chance of getting the car.

Being Queen

Queen Elizabeth does not hold a passport. Since all British passports are issued in the queen's name, she herself doesn't need one.

And though Queen Elizabeth drove a truck in World War Two as a member of the armed services; she also doesn't require a driver's license.

Queen Elizabeth sent her first email in 1976 while taking part in a network technology demonstration at the Royal Signals and Radar Establishment, a research facility in Malvern, England.

Queen Elizabeth owns all unmarked mute swans in open water, but only exercises ownership on certain stretches of the River Thames and its surrounding tributaries.

Swans

Not only are swans monogamous but male swans play an active role in building nests and incubating eggs.

McDonalds or Golden Arches Theory of Conflict Prevention

The Golden Arches Theory of Conflict Prevention states that no two countries with a McDonalds have gone to war with each other. This unfortunately didn't even have any truth even when it was first published in 1999 as Panama had its first McDonald's franchise in 1971 and was subsequently invaded by the United States in 1989. There have been more notable exceptions since then.

The background to why this claim was asserted does contain some truth McDonald's, like any large corporation, tends to do a lot of research before moving into a new territory as for a country to have a market for fast food a solid infrastructure and a certain degree of development is required.

Microwave Oven

The microwave oven was invented by Percy Spencer who was standing in front of an active radar set when he noticed the candy bar he had in his pocket had melted. Spencer though not the first person to notice this he was the first to investigate it.

After the chocolate bar experience, he started experimenting with other food including popcorn kernels, which became the world's first microwaved popcorn.

He then decided to cut a hole in the side of a kettle, put a whole egg in the kettle and positioned the magnetron to direct the microwaves into the hole. This crude mechanism exploded egg in the face of one of his co-workers, who was observing his experiment.

Spencer created the first true microwave oven by attaching a high density electromagnetic field generator to an enclosed metal box. The magnetron emitted microwaves into the metal box blocking any escape, allowing for controlled and safe experimentation. He then placed various food items in the box, while observing effects and monitoring temperatures.

It was in 1967 that the first relatively affordable ($495) and reasonably sized (countertop) microwave oven was put on sale.

Russia once ran out of vodka

On 9th May 1945 Nazi Germany officially surrendered to the Soviet Union. Soviet citizens immediately took to the streets to celebrate and by the time Joseph Stalin addressed the nation 22 hours later the entire country had run out of vodka!

999 (emergency telephone number)

999 is the historic emergency number for the United Kingdom, but calls are also accepted on both the European Union emergency number, 112, and the United States emergency number, 911. In both these cases, calls are diverted to the regular 999 service.

First introduced in the London area on 30 June 1937, the UK's 999 number is the world's oldest emergency call service. The system was introduced following a fire on 10 November 1935 in a house on Wimpole Street in which five women were killed. A neighbour had tried to telephone the fire brigade and was so outraged at being held in a queue by the Welbeck telephone exchange that he wrote a letter to the editor of The Times, which prompted a government inquiry.

The 9-9-9 format was chosen based on the 'button A' and 'button B' design of prepayment coin-operated public payphones in wide use (first introduced in 1925) which could be easily modified to allow free use of the 9 digit on the rotary dial in addition to the 0 digit (then used to call the operator), without allowing free use of numbers involving other digits.

As it happens, the choice of 999 was fortunate for accessibility reasons, compared with e.g. lower numbers: in the dark or in dense smoke, 999 could be dialled by placing a finger one hole away from the dial stop and rotating the dial to the full extent three times.

<u>Bus to nowhere</u>

Many nursing homes for the elderly in Germany have taken to putting in place fake bus stops outside their establishments to help prevent patients with Alzheimer's from wandering off and getting lost.

<u>Hyperlexia</u>

Hyperlexia is defined as the precocious ability to read words without prior training. Hyperlexics often learn to read before the age of 5.

<u>Reindeer</u>

Reindeer are believed to be the only mammals than can see ultraviolet light. This adaptation allows them to see things in the harsh white of the Arctic that they would otherwise miss.

Strange rules of the roads

On Estonia's ice roads it is illegal to wear a seatbelt as to do so would hinder your ability to escape, or to drive between 25 km/h and 40 km/h as to do so would create dangerous vibrations that could crack the surface of the road.

McDonalds

Dick and Mac McDonald founded McDonalds but sold the name and rights to Raymond Kroc, they renamed their original restaurant The Big M which was subsequently put out of business by a McDonalds Raymond Kroc opened just across the street.

The Intrepid aircraft carrier which is now a floating museum in New York has a McDonalds on board.

The first Ronald McDonald was fired for becoming too fat.

The average McDonalds in the US has an annual turnover of over $2.5 million which is over double that of it's rival Burger King.

Over 10% of McDonalds turnover comes from Happy Meals.

Though McDonalds tend to be pretty generic one in New Zealand is partly made out of a decommissioned DC3 plane.

Audio cues on the Moscow Metro

On the Moscow Metro circular line, the train coming from the centre has a female announcer and the train going to the centre has a male announcer.

Big Mac Index

The Big Mac index was invented by The Economist magazine in 1986 as a light-hearted attempt to gauge whether currencies are at their correct exchange level.

Burgernomics was never intended to be taken too seriously but managed to become a global standard all the same.

It has been used in several economics textbooks and been the subject for many academic studies.

<u>Empire State Building</u>

In 1945 the Empire State building survived the impact from a North American Aviation B-25 bomber. The crash killed 14 including both of the plane's pilots and sole passenger and 11 workers in the Empire State building.

The B-25 was flying from New Bedford, Massachusetts to La Guardia Airport in New York City in very heavy fog. The flight path brought the plane slowly and directly over Manhattan. The plane was flying at a low enough altitude that the pilot had to swerve to avoid the Chrysler Building but in doing so it instead hit the north side of the Empire State Building, near the 79th floor.

Upon impact the plane's fuel ignited and caused a fire which engulfed a number of floors. One engine detached and went straight through the building and landed in a penthouse apartment across the street. The other engine also detached and severed the lifting cables of two elevators on the 79th floor, causing the elevators to rapidly descend to the sub basement. An elevator operator Betty Lou Oliver inside at the time survived this fall of 75 stories and this descent still stands as the Guinness World Record for the longest survived elevator fall ever recorded. Other plane parts ended up in and on top of nearby buildings.

A lasting impacts of the incident were the passing of the United States Federal Tort Claims Act of 1946 which gave American citizens the right to sue the federal government.

Once a woman attempted to commit suicide by jumping out of the Empire State Building, however a strong gust blew her back albeit one floor lower. A security guard rescued her and her only injuries were a broken hip.

It is possible for an individual to own part of the Empire State Building by purchasing shares in the Real Estate Investment Trust - Empire State Realty Trust which floated on the market in 2013. Ticker symbol ESRT

The Empire State Building hosts annual Urban Camp Outs for scouts whereby they can stay overnight on the 86th Floor.

Rock stars and candy

Van Halen's standard performance contract contained a condition that there be no brown M & Ms in the back stage area. Rather than being artists with an over inflated sense of their own importance the condition was there for the very practical reason of ensuring that all the terms of their complex production contract had been read and understood.

Van Halen had a much more complex setup than other bands at that time, the contract was interspersed with a few conditions like the "no brown M & Ms" so that simple checks could be made to see that the setup had been done correctly.

No left turns strategy

United Parcel Services or UPS, is a global package delivery company. To drive operational efficiency, they adopted a right turn only strategy, UPS plots its delivery routes to make as many right turns as possible. In a world where half the driving choices are left turns, they avoid turning left as much as possible.

Ship Tunnel

The Stad Ship Tunnel is a proposed canal and tunnel to bypass the Stad peninsula in Selje, Norway. The peninsula is one of the most exposed and dangerous areas of the Norwegian coast.

The tunnel was included in the National Transport Plan in 2013. The tunnel will be 45 metres high and 36 metres wide, with water to a depth of 12 metres and will be able to handle ships of up to 16,000 tonnes.

Shakespeare

The Knock-Knock joke was first seen in William Shakespeare's Macbeth.

Hashima

Hashima a ghost island off the Japanese coast that served as the inspiration for the lair of villain Raoul Silva in the James Bond movie Skyfall. The island was populated from 1887 to 1974 as a coal mining facility but has now fallen into a state of dereliction.

The Decimation of decimation

Decimation was a form of military discipline used by senior commanders in the Roman Army to punish units or large groups guilty of capital offences such as mutiny or desertion. The word decimation is derived from Latin meaning "removal of a tenth" the modern day meaning though has become to destroy or kill a large part of a group

Burning bridges

Burning bridges is the act of eliminating all possibility of return or retreat. The Romans were said to do just that when invading hostile territory. If boats or bridges were used to cross a river, a commander would order they be burnt, so that there would be no option of turning back or retreating. Knowing that there was no option of retreat boosted the motivation of attacking soldiers.

Samhain

Samhain is a Gaelic festival marking the end of the harvest season and the beginning of winter or the "darker half" of the year.

Calling shotgun

Calling "Shotgun" is the act of claiming the front passenger seat of a car for one's self. The history of calling "Shotgun" goes back to the days of covered wagons and the Wild West.

On a trip across the Wild West, the driver of a wagon would have to concentrate on holding the reins of and guiding his horse team. This left him and the occupants of his wagon susceptible to attacks from bandits and thieves. To counteract this risk a guard would sit next to the driver with a shotgun and fend off the enemy.

Fastest Rollercoaster

The fastest rollercoaster in the world is the Intamin built 240 km/h Formula Rossa in Ferrari World United Arab Emirates.

The Intamin brand name is an abbreviation for: INTernational AMusement INstallations.

Holocaust memorial Berlin

The Degussa company's involvement (providing the anti-graffiti substance Protectosil used to cover the stelae) with the construction of the Holocaust memorial in Berlin was controversial because the company had previously been involved in various ways in the Nazi persecution of the Jews. A subsidiary company of Degussa, Degesch, produced the Zyklon B gas used to poison people in the gas chambers.

Molotov cocktail

The Molotov cocktail, also known as a Petrol Bomb, Fire Bomb or just Molotov is a generic name used for a variety of improvised incendiary weapons. They are easily produced and hence frequently used by protesters and fighters in urban guerrilla warfare.

The name was coined by the Finns poking fun at the Soviet politician Molotov and his propaganda broadcasts.

First Car phone

The first car phone was the Bell System which weighed 36 kg and was first used in St. Louis on 17th June 1946.

1984

The United Kingdom has an estimated 4.2 million closed circuit television or CCTV cameras - one for every 14 people in the country and 20% of CCTV cameras globally. It has been calculated that each person in the United Kingdom is caught on camera on an average of 300 times daily.

George Orwell's (of Big Brother and 1984 fame) flat in Islington North London where he lived until his death in 1950, is surrounded by upwards of 30 CCTV cameras!

After the London terrorist attacks on the 7th July 2005 police used CCTV footage to trace the bombers back to where they lived.

Botulinum toxin

Botulinum toxin can cause botulism, a serious and life-threatening illness in humans and animals. However, nowadays many humans routinely have one of the three forms of botulinum toxin type A or one form of botulinum toxin type B injected as part of various cosmetic and medical procedures. These are known under various trade names such as Botox, Dysport, Xeomin and MyoBloc, etc.

Airport security

A British charity is advising children being forced into arranged marriages to fight back with metal spoons. Forced child marriages don't often happen within the UK so girls who are being compelled by their families to marry a stranger are usually flown to another country where the union can occur.

Thanks to heightened security measures when airport security detects metal objects hidden under travellers clothing, they're taken away to a private screening area, and in the scenario outlined above the children have the chance to tell an authority figure that they are being shipped abroad to marry a stranger.

PARC

PARC (Palo Alto Research Center Incorporated), formerly Xerox PARC, is a legendary research and development company located in Palo Alto, California.

It was here that many of the technological innovations that we take for granted were invented.

These include:
The Graphical user interface or GUI, featuring windows and icons, operated with a mouse
The What you see is what you get or WYSIWYG text editor
Interpress, a resolution-independent graphical page-description language and the precursor to PostScript
Ethernet as a local-area computer network
Fully formed object-oriented programming in the Smalltalk programming language and integrated development environment.
Model–view–controller software architecture
Laser printers,
Computer-generated bitmap graphics

PARC was at one-time Intel's biggest customer, due to it's insatiable demand for memory for it's pioneering Alto workstation.

Nintendo epilepsy ads

When the "Electric Soldier Porygon" episode of the Pokémon animated series was broadcast in Japan it triggered an epileptic fit in a considerable number of the children due to strobe type effects in the episode.

It's estimated that around 1 in 4000 people are vulnerable to "photosensitive seizures" and other health issues when viewing strobe lighting and this particular program had over 4 million viewers.

It triggered additional epileptic fits in some viewers of a later television news report about the event. Foolishly extracts with the strobe effects from the episode were included in the report.

Nobel Peace Prize

Hitler, Mussolini and Stalin were all nominated for the Nobel Peace Prize

Vanity Licence Plates

Vanity licence plates were introduced by the State of Connecticut in the United States as a reward for drivers with 5 years of accident free driving.

The first geek vanity licence plate was the Live Free or Die UNIX plate.

The DeLorean in Back to the Future features a vanity plate "Outatime".

Credit Card test numbers

There is a list of test credit card numbers provided by credit card companies that will successfully authenticate, these are used for testing payment card systems both on and offline.

Credit Card font

Traditionally credit cards use the Farrington B numeric font, it dates back to the first usage of Optical Character Recognition or OCR. The first application of OCR was reading credit cards at gas stations in the US and recognition was more reliable on a simple and open font like Farrington B. Today the information is instead read from the magnetic stripe on the back of the card.

PlayStation supercomputer

It was alleged that in December 2000 Iraq bought 4000 Sony PlayStation 2s with the hope of building a clustered supercomputer.

Code talkers

Code talkers are people who used obscure languages as a means of secret communication during wartime.

The most famous of which were United States soldiers during the two World Wars who used their knowledge of a Native American languages as a basis to transmit coded messages.

Code talkers transmitted these messages over military telephone or radio communications networks using formal or informally developed codes built upon their native languages.

Enron

Enron did not pay taxes in four of the five years before its collapse, according to the financial statements it sent to shareholders.

To avoid taxes, it created 881 offshore subsidiaries, 692 of them in the Cayman Islands.

Catholic Church

As an organisation the Catholic church has survived for over 2000 years.

It has no more than 5 levels of hierarchy and members are not allowed to have heirs so that wealth remains within the organisation.

Scavi

Under Saint Peter's Basilica in Rome, Italy there are excavations (or scavi) that one can visit as long as you reserve a place and buy a ticket in advance.

The scavi are made up of a Roman necropolis (city of the dead) and many graves of the various Popes including the first Pope Saint Peter.

Prancing horses

The traffic lights in Maranello Italy the home town of the Ferrari factory are shaped like prancing horses rather than the regular circular ones.

Shipping and pollution

The shipping industry produces almost twice as much CO_2 as the much maligned aviation industry. The oil it typically burns (residual) also has a much higher sulphur and heavy metals content than the lighter oils used for aviation.

Isle of Man

The Isle of Man also known simply as Mann, is a self-governing British Crown Dependency, located in the Irish Sea between Great Britain and Ireland.

The head of state is Queen Elizabeth II, who holds the title of Lord of Mann. The Tynwald (or government) is the oldest continuous government in the world.

The roads there have no speed limit and are home to one of the most prestigious motorcycle races in the world - The Isle of Man TT.

The Isle of Man it is also famous for a breed of tailless cats and almost tail less cats.

Cowfriends

Like humans, cows have best friends with whom they form close friendships. Cows choose to exclusively spend time with these 2 to 4 best friends. They also hold grudges for years and may dislike particular individuals.

Cow's spots are as unique as a fingerprint and no two cows have exactly the same pattern of spots.

Wal Mart

Wal Mart has over 9,000 stores across the 50 states of the US but none in any of New York's 5 boroughs.

Palace of the People

The Palace of the Parliament in Bucharest is the world's largest administrative civilian building, most expensive administrative building and heaviest building. It was built by Romanian's megalomaniac former dictator Nicolae Ceauş escu.

Nürburgring

The Nürburgring is a motorsports complex around the village of Nürburg, Rhineland-Palatinate, Germany. It features a Grand Prix race track built in 1984, and a much longer old "North loop" track which was built in the 1920s around the village and medieval castle of Nürburg in the Eifel mountains.

The north loop or Nordschleife is 20.8 km long and there is a 300 metres difference of elevation from its lowest to highest points.

Jackie Stewart nicknamed it "The Green Hell," and it is widely considered to be the most demanding and difficult purpose-built racing circuit in the world

On many occasions throughout the year anyone with a road-legal vehicle can complete an almost full lap of the Nordschleife circuit by simply paying a toll.

Orange blue contrast

If one looks at contemporary movie posters it will be seen that many include the contrasting colours of orange and blue. Humans have been shown to be particularly attentive to these colours in advertising.

Chess boxing

A new sport combines the athleticism of boxing with the cerebralism of chess. A knockout in the ring or checkmate on the board signal a victory. Failing that points are scored for both!

Cheese

The Swiss cheese Emmental gets its characteristic holes from gas released by bacteria during it's creation. All cheeses contain these bacteria which produce the lactic acid necessary to create the edible final product. The bacteria P. shermani, releases carbon dioxide when it consumes the lactic acid and creates bubbles and these bubbles form little air pockets, resulting in the characteristic holes in the Swiss cheese.

Blue cheese is formed when a specific type of mould is added during the cheese making process and an additional step in the ageing process called needling. The most widely used moulds in blue-veined cheeses are Penicillium Roqueforti and Penicillium Glaucum. These fungi are found commonly in nature and were first discovered when cheese makers started ageing their cheeses in damp, cool caves.

MIT Museum

MIT the world leading science and engineering university has a small museum, part of which celebrates the various hacks it's students perpetrated on their own institution and against their arch rivals Harvard.

An example of the former is when MIT's Green Building was turned into a giant game of Tetris and one of the most famous of the latter was when a hot air balloon was launched from their arch-rival Harvard's playing field during a football game.

Gaudi

Gaudi was a revolutionary modernist architect from Reus in Spain.

Gaudí's works reflect his highly individual and distinctive style and are largely concentrated in Barcelona most notably his magnum opus the Sagrada Família.

Seven of his works to date have been declared World Heritage Sites by UNESCO.

The Sagrada Família Gaudi's iconic church in Barcelona has been under construction since 1882 with construction anticipated to be completed in 2026, the centenary of Gaudí's death.

Printer ink

By volume most printer ink in replacement cartridges is more expensive than champagne.

Boomerang

The boomerangs synonymous with Australian Aboriginals date from at least ten thousand years ago but they are not the oldest examples in the world. For example, a boomerang found in Jaskinia Obłazowa in the Carpathian Mountains in Poland is believed to date from thirty thousand years ago.

Smartphone

The first smartphone was invented in 1993 by IBM, it had a touch screen and combined a mobile phone, pager, PDA, and fax machine.

Typewriters

The layout of a typewriter was designed to slow down typists as fast typing was causing early typewriters to fail. Several attempts have since been made to switch to more efficient layouts like Dvorak but the QWERTY layout is still the most prevalent.

Heroin trademark

In 1895, the German drug company Bayer marketed diacetylmorphine as an over-the-counter drug under the trademark name Heroin.

Aspirin

It's highly likely that if aspirin were discovered today it would most likely not get regulatory approval or would be approved as a prescription only drug due to it's well documented gastrointestinal side effects.

Oktoberfest

The famous Munich Oktoberfest is actually held at the end of September.

Stasi

The GDR or German Democratic Republic had one of the most effective and repressive intelligence and secret police agencies to ever have existed. It was known more commonly as the Stasi.

Its main task was spying on the GDR's citizens, and utilised a vast number of it's own citizens to act as informants. It fought any opposition by both overt and covert measures.

One of it's most sinister methods was the psychological destruction of dissidents. The Stasi would break into homes and rearrange the contents to make their victims question their own sanity and or to show they could come in and out at will.

The ratio of Stasi full time Stasi agents to GDR citizens was approximately 1:165.

The Stasi even kept a database of sweat from people they questioned. These samples were collected by putting a piece of material on a chair when they were interrogating people.

Panopticon

The Panopticon is a type of institutional building conceived by the Englishman Jeremy Bentham in the late 18th century.

The design allows for a single observer to observe all inmates of an institution without the inmates being able to tell whether they are being observed or not.

Modern call centre and office buildings intentionally follow the same design with workers feeling like they are being observed whether they are or not.

Isaac Newton

Being monumentally intelligent and one of the most influential scientists of all time did not prevent Isaac Newton from losing his fortune speculating on the South Sea Company.

Interrobang

The interrobang is a nonstandard punctuation mark used in various written languages and intended to combine the functions of the question mark and the exclamation mark.

Superhero window cleaners

Window cleaners in children's hospitals have taken to wearing super hero costumes to cheer the patients.

Bordeaux

The vine was introduced to the Bordeaux region of France by the Romans in the mid-1st century and wine production has continued in the region since then.

Vatican

The world's smallest country is the Vatican City with a total area of 0.44 sq. km or .17 sq. miles and its official language is Latin.

The Vatican City mints its own euros, prints its own stamps, issues passports and license plates, operates media outlets and has its own flag and anthem.

It has a small army (the Swiss guard) which is composed entirely of Swiss citizens.

Nintendo

Nintendo was founded in 1889 as a manufacturer of playing cards and it wasn't until 1978 that it made it's first computer game.

The Legend of Zelda was the first console game to allow a player to save their progress.

In Super Monkey Ball it is possible to land on the pontoons in the sea.

Fire hydrant

It is not known who invented the fire hydrant because the patent for it was lost in a fire at the patent office in Washington DC in 1836.

Ford

Though he popularised and refined it Henry Ford didn't invent the assembly line.

Before the advent of computers Ford Motor Company used to weigh invoices to estimate how much money it owed to it's suppliers, it was surprisingly accurate.

Wombat

Wombat poo is cube shaped.

Titanic

Titanic the ship cost less to make than Titanic the movie.

Flying first class across the Atlantic is today about the same in dollars as it was to travel first class on the Titanic then, and much much less in real terms.

Keeping true to the principle of "Women and children first", the percentage of passengers that survived the Titanic was 75%, 52% and 21% for women, children and men respectfully.

Triple Witching

Triple witching occurs on the third Friday of March, June, September and December. This is when on the same day the contracts for stock index futures, stock index options and stock options all expire.

Bloodhound

A bloodhound's nose is about three thousand times more sensitive than a human's nose.

Snipers

Snipers are trained to shoot between heartbeats so the blood flow to their fingers doesn't put them off when aiming and shooting.

A British sniper serving in Afghanistan killed six with one bullet when he hit the trigger switch which detonated a suicide bomber's bomb.

The worlds most successful sniper was Finn Simo Häyhä. He is officially credited with 540 sniper kills (with unofficial numbers well over 800). More remarkable is that that Simo achieved all this in just 100 days and alone.

New York Gold

The streets of New York may not be paved in gold but massive basement vaults belonging to the Federal Reserve Bank of New York's house the world's largest known depository of monetary gold. At its peak, the vault contained over 12,000 tons of gold.

Gold bars

Gold bars are not 100 percent pure gold because they would be too malleable to preserve their shape and would be difficult to store or move. Instead each bar contains a small amount of at least one other metal, such as copper, silver or platinum.

New York Nitrogen Tanks

Nitrogen is often used by telephone companies in New York City to pressurise underground cables in an effort to drive out moisture. The tanks can sometimes be seen on the streets of New York.

Star Wars

Darth Vader was portrayed by three actors in the original 3 films James Earl Jones for the voice, Sebastian Shaw for the face and David Prowse for the body.

The characteristic sound of the voice was achieved by using a SCUBA regulator.

Frank Oz voiced Yoda and he was also the voice of Miss Piggy from the Muppets

The characteristic Tie Fighter sound was created by combining the call of an elephant and the sound of a car been driven on wet pavement.

Dutch Courage

Dutch courage refers to artificially stimulated courage especially that gained from intoxication from alcohol.

Peace Sign

The ubiquitous peace sign is made of the juxtaposed semaphore signals for N and D an abbreviation for Nuclear Disarmament

Twitter

Twitter's original 140-character limit on tweets was derived from the SMS mobile phone messaging service. This was divided up as 20 characters for the username and 140 characters for the message, this allowed tweets to be delivered via a single SMS without any issues with split messages.

The idea for Twitter's hashtags came from a Twitter user Chris Messina.

DeLorean

The DeLorean was a sports car manufactured in Belfast, Ireland for the American market from 1981 to early 1983.

Only 9000 DeLoreans were ever produced but it achieved cult status in popular culture due to its appearance as a modified time machine in the Back to the Future film trilogy.

In Back to the Future it featured the vanity license plate "Outatime".

Stuxnet

Stuxnet is a computer virus believed to have been specifically created by United States and Israel intelligence agencies to attack Iran's nuclear production facilities.

Stuxnet's modus operandi is to initially first via Microsoft Windows, and then subsequently by specifically targeting Siemens industrial control systems.

These particular Siemens control systems were used to control Iranian centrifuges used to purify the radioactive raw materials.

Piggly Wiggly

The first supermarket Piggly Wiggly was founded in Memphis Tennessee in 1916.

It introduced many of the innovations we take for granted in modern supermarkets such as checkout stands and price stickers on every item. It was the first supermarket to provide shopping trolleys for customers in 1937.

Lucy in the Sky with Diamonds

The Beatles song title Lucy in the Sky with Diamonds apparently spelling out LSD was denied by both Lennon and McCartney. Lennon's claimed the inspiration for the song came when his son, Julian, showed him a nursery school drawing he called "Lucy - in the Sky with Diamonds"

Dark Side of the Rainbow

Dark Side of the Rainbow refers to the phenomenon of pairing the 1973 Pink Floyd album The Dark Side of the Moon with the visual portion of the 1939 film The Wizard of Oz." At many points the film and album seem to be in sync. The band dismiss the idea that there is any relationship between the album and the movie.

Beatles

The Beatles were famously turned down by Decca Record who were looking to sign a new Beat group. The Beatles auditioned at Decca Studios in West Hampstead, North London, UK, but in what is considered to be one of the biggest mistakes in music history, Decca decided to reject the band and instead plumped for Brian Poole and the Tremeloes. Though the Tremeloes were successful in their own right their success paled in comparison to the Beatles.

<u>Natural highs</u>

Human's aren't the only creatures to enjoy recreational drugs. Elephants and monkey's both imbibe alcohol filled fruit, horses consume hallucinogenic weeds and big horn sheep have a particular fondness for narcotic lichens.

Scientists now believe that dolphins are members of this club as dolphins have recently been observed playing gently with pufferfish in order to provoke them into unleashing their chemical defence mechanism. The chemical released by the pufferfish induces a trance like state in the dolphins.

<u>Iceman</u>

The profession of Iceman was common in the late 19th century to mid 20th century. Icemen make daily deliveries of ice for iceboxes which were common before the advent of the refrigerator.

The ice he delivered was stored from the previous winter or transported from a colder climate.

<u>Canned food</u>

The technique of canning food came about when the French government offered a substantial cash prize for the discovery of a new way to preserve food in 1795. This was eventually won in 1810 by a French man named Appert who invented a means of heat treating and bottling foodstuffs.

Around the same time an English man Peter Durand patented a method of preserving food in a tin can, one which is used to this day.

Tin cans originally required a hammer and chisel to open and did not really take off up until the invention of the can opener by an Englishman named Yates in 1855.

Submarine

Submarine crews usually wear sneakers or other soft bottomed shoes when at sea as even small sounds can give away a submarines position to an enemy.

Kangaroo

In a process known as diapause a kangaroo can pause her pregnancy in times of drought for up to 2 years.

Michelin Guide

In 1900 the tyre manufacturers Michelin published the first edition of a guide for French motorists. The guide was intended to boost the demand for cars and driving and hence car tyres.

The first edition had a print run of 35,000 and was given away for free. The guide contained information for motorists such as maps, locations of garages, places to stay, places to eat and of course instructions for repairing and changing tyres.

The restaurant section became more and more popular so a team of inspectors was hired to visit and review restaurants specifically for the guide.

The 1926 edition of the guide was the first to award stars for fine dining.

The 1931 edition debuted the hierarchy of one, two and three stars which continues to this day.

Michelin inspectors are completely anonymous and their meals and expenses are paid for solely by Michelin.

The Smellies

In an attempt to compete with the introduction of television the cinema industry introduced competing smell technologies such as Smell-O-Vision, Smell-O-Rama and AromaRama. These systems released odours during the projection of a movie so that the cinemagoers could smell what was happening in the plot line of the movie and thus make the experience more immersive.

Utilising the Smell-O-Vision technology the 1960 film Scent of Mystery released 30 odours during the screening of the movie. Due to technological and financial reasons smell technology never took off but Disney still use it in some of the attractions at their theme parks.

Whiffling

Whiffling is an ornithological term describing the rapid descent of a bird with a zig-zagging, side-slipping motion.

At some points during the whiffling process, the birds body is inverted but its neck and head are twisted 180 degrees around versus the normal position, this also inverts the aerodynamics force so instead of generating lift bird plummets toward the ground for a brief period of time before righting itself. This erratic evasive motion is used to avoid predators of an avian or human nature.

February 30th

In February 1712 Sweden had two leap days added to it's calendar. This was the only occurrence of February 30th in history.

Railway Guns

Schwerer Gustav and Dora were the names of two German 80 cm railway guns. They were built by Krupp in the late 1930s. Fully assembled the guns weighed circa 1,350 tonnes, and could fire shells weighing seven tonnes to a range of 47 kilometres.

Loudest band in the World

Pioneering English House/Electronica band Leftfield developed a reputation for having very loud live shows. In June 1996 while on tour to publicise their debut album Leftism they played a gig at Brixton Academy. The volume of the sound system caused dust and plaster to fall from the ceiling. The volume was recorded at 137 dB.

Landing a plane with only one wing

An Israeli pilot Ziv Nedivi once landed a F-15 Eagle fighter plane with only one wing.

During an air combat training session Nedivi's F-15 collided with an A-4 Skyhawk and the right wing of the F-15 Eagle was sheared off roughly 60 cm from the fuselage. Due to leaking fuel and vapour Nedivi was not aware of the catastrophic damage his plane had suffered.

To counteract the spin after the collision Nedivi engaged the afterburner to increase speed, allowing him to regain control of the aircraft. He was able to prevent stalling and maintain control because of the lift generated by the large horizontal surface area of the fuselage, the stabilators and remaining wing areas.

Ultimately he landed the F-15 at twice the normal speed, the high landing speed was required to maintain the necessary lift.

Efficient boarding

Though boarding planes by letter rather than row (for example window row A first) has been found to be more efficient, it is not used as people often have travelling companions and or children and do not want to be separated from them even briefly.

Train Stuffers

Tokyo's Subway and Suburban lines get so busy at times that the Station Attendants or Conductor's have to physically stuff passengers on to trains. The overcrowding of trains has also led to the introduction of women only carriages.

Breakfast Candy

Some modern day breakfast cereals are over 50% sugar, and historically some have had up to 70% sugar. They are marketed as "cereals" as "Breakfast sugars" or "breakfast candy" doesn't have quite the same ring to it!

Lego or Legos?

In the United Kingdom the toy is commonly called Lego and in the United States it's commonly called Legos but in fact both are incorrect as "Lego" is an adjective so it should be used as follows Lego bricks, Lego building, Lego products, etc.

JRR Tolkien

JRR Tolkien writer of The Lord of the Rings trilogy got his inspiration for the epic fantasy battle scenes from his first hand experiences of trench warfare World War 1.

Mismatch

The founder of Match.com the dating website lost his girlfriend to another man she met on Match.com

Marking their territory

Cat's have scent glands in their paw pads, cheeks, and head so when the knead us they are not showing us affection but merely marking out their territory.

Walkman 3000

Sony predicted that by the year 3,000 that the iconic Walkman would be wearing their users. Sadly, for Sony they largely missed an industry wide shift to MP3 players!

Porsche

The first car designed by Ferdinand Porsche was an electric car called the P1 for carmaker Jacob Lohner in 1898. The P1 had a top speed of 34 km/h and a range of 80km.

Porsche also designed the Volkswagen Beetle which shares a number of key characteristics with the iconic 911 such as a rear air cooled engine driving mostly the rear wheels in a coupe format.

221B Baker Street

221B Baker Street, London is the address of author Sir Arthur Conan Doyle's fictional creation detective Sherlock Holmes.

When the Sherlock Holmes stories were first published there was no number 221 on Baker Street but later Baker Street was extended to include 221.

In 1932 the Abbey National Building Society moved into the premises that spanned numbers 219 through 229 and such was the volume of correspondence addressed to Sherlock Holmes that for a long time they employed a full-time secretary to answer it.

Vitamin D

One theory for the variation in skin colour in humans is that it is a genetic adaptation related to the ability to synthesise Vitamin D. As people with red hair tend to also have pale skin they are more efficient at making vitamin D and do not need so much sunlight in order to get the amount they need.

South Africa

The security situation in South Africa is so extreme that it has over 9,000 private security firms employing more than 400,000 country wide. This total is more than the combined forces of the police and army.

Low cost supermarkets

Low cost supermarkets like Aldi, Lidl, Trader Joes, etc. manage to have lower costs by limiting the items they sell. Typically, they would sell ~ 1000 items as opposed to the 25,000 – 50,000 that Tesco or Wal-Mart would sell.

Often they carry only one brand in a particular category. This allows them to manage their supply chain much more efficiently. With just one brand in each category they can accurately predict sales, and due to the high sales volume they can deal directly with manufacturers and source very high quality products and negotiate volume discounts.

Another key factor in their success is their ranges of own label goods which can achieve the same supply chain efficiencies. Additionally, these own label products do not incur marketing or advertising costs, and contribute towards distribution costs. As an example Trader Joe's carries 90% private label products.

This vertical integration and control of retailing, wholesaling, distribution and manufacturing allows them to add the margin where it is most prudent to do so.

Lazy intelligent

Kurt von Hammerstein-Equord was a German general who served for a period as Commander-in-Chief of the Reichswehr (German Military Administration). He is famous both for being an ardent opponent of Hitler and the Nazi regime and for making a major contribution to the field of performance management.

As Chief of the Army High Command, Hammerstein-Equord oversaw the composition of the German manual on military unit command and in this he famously divided his officers into four groups clever, diligent, stupid, and lazy officers.

Usually two characteristics are combined.

The clever and diligent he felt had their place is the General Staff. He consigned the stupid and lazy (which make up 90 percent of every army) to routine duties.

He believed anyone who is both clever and lazy is most qualified for the highest leadership duties, because they possess the intellectual clarity and the composure necessary for difficult decisions.

He had least regard for the stupid and diligent, he felt these caused only mischief and did most harm to an organisation.

<u>Disney Race</u>

Disney has a program called Run Disney where athletes can compete in races of varying distances within it's theme parks. One such event the Walt Disney World Marathon goes through all four Walt Disney World Theme Parks.

<u>Egalitarian executive</u>

Where as historically many company executives set themselves apart with lavish perks Intel's Andrew Grove eschewed these. He sharing a similar cubicle to all other company employees (the only concession as CEO was that he had some additional file storage space).

This trend has intensified recently with many companies eliminating cubicles and going with completely open plan office areas.

<u>Switzerland</u>

Switzerland's official name is Confoederatio Helvetica hence the abbreviation CH

Despite being neutral Switzerland has space in a public or private bomb shelter for each one of it's citizens.

Switzerland only granted women the right to vote at a Federal level in 1971 with one canton Appenzell Innerrhoden not granting women the vote on local issues until 1991 (and then only having been forced to by the Swiss Federal Supreme Court.

Swiss army knife

The Swiss army knife is a brand of pocket knife or multi-tool manufactured by one of two companies Victorinox AG or Wenger SA. The term "Swiss Army knife" was coined by US soldiers after World War II due to the difficulty they had in pronouncing the German name.

The Swiss Army knife generally has a sharp blade, as well as various tools, such as screwdrivers, a can opener, etc. These attachments are stowed inside the handle of the knife through a pivot point mechanism. The handle is usually red, and features a Victorinox or Wenger "cross" logo or, for Swiss military issue knives, the coat of arms of Switzerland.

Tacoma Narrows Bridge

The Tacoma Narrows Bridge spanned the Tacoma Narrows strait of Puget Sound between Tacoma and the Kitsap Peninsula, Washington State, in the United States.

The Tacoma Narrows Bridge collapsed on November 7, 1940, as a result of aeroelastic flutter caused by a 68 km/h wind. The bridge collapse had lasting effects on science and engineering and is featured in many physics texts as a cautionary tale.

Odd Museums

The Cork, Ireland Butter Museum commemorates what was once the world's largest butter market.

The Wimbledon Lawn Tennis Museum in London explores the game's evolution from a garden party pastime to a multimillion dollar professional sport played worldwide and includes an extensive, unsurpassed collection of tennis memorabilia dating back to 1555

The worlds smallest Titanic museum used take up 1.45 square meters of Lisa Maria Schwödiauer's bathroom in Linz, Austria. It has now been relocated to the kitchen of her new house.

The Museum of Bad Art located in Massachusetts, USA curates it's collection based on the idea that museums are too biased towards talented artists and seek to redress this inequality.

The Winchester Mystery House was built by Sarah Winchester, wife and widow of William Wirt Winchester, the heir to the Winchester Rifle fortune. The house was built in a haphazard manner and was supposedly to accommodate the souls of those killed by Winchester rifles.

The Story of Berlin Museum includes a the still-functioning underground nuclear bomb shelter.

The Museum of Funeral Carriages, Barcelona has visitors report to the city's Municipal Funeral Services from where they will be guided to the basement by a security guard and the exhibition unlocked.

The Paris Sewers Museum lets you learn about the history of the hygiene of Paris.

<u>Love all</u>

The tennis scoring term "love" is said to come from the English phrase "neither for love nor for money", indicating nothing and the proper way to describe a score of zero to zero is to say love-all.

Swords and suits of armour

Suits of armour used weigh up to 25 kg and they considerably restricted the wearers mobility.

Swords were also very heavy and most injuries were caused by a bludgeoning effect due to their weight rather than a cutting effect due to their sharpness.

Military salutes

The modern military salute originated in the Middle Ages when knights greeted each other by raising their visors to show their faces, this upward movement of the hand lingers on today as the salute.

99

There are two competing theories as to why many prices in shops end in 99. One is a psychological pricing scheme used by retailers to make products seem one dollar less expensive than they really are i.e. $1.99 rather than $2 The other is as an anti theft measure; forcing store clerks to ring up orders and open cash drawers (to give customers their one cent change); rather than just pocketing the money.

Kevlar

Kevlar is the registered trademark for a high strength synthetic fibre first developed by DuPont in 1965.

Typically, it is spun into ropes or fabric sheets that can be used as is or as an ingredient in composite material components.

It's first commercial application was as a replacement for steel in racing tires.

Modern day applications include inclusion in bicycle tires, racing sails and body armour.

Spider web

Spider silk is a much less dense material than steel so for a given weight of spider silk it is five times as strong as the same weight of steel.

Ancient animals

Galapagos Tortoises can live for over 170 years, Bowhead whales can live for more than 200 years and the ocean quahog (a species of edible clam) can live for over 400 years.

Starbucks

Starbucks is named after a character from Moby Dick.

To date there are no Starbucks cafes in Italy. This is set to change with the first due to open in Milan in 2018.

It is possible to see some Starbucks outlets while sitting in another one.

Starbucks opens ten minutes before it's posted opening times and shuts ten minutes after it's posted closing times in order to facilitate its customers.

The Peet's and Starbucks chains have a shared heritage with Alfred Peet supplying the initial Starbucks coffee shop with coffee

Starbucks spends more on healthcare for it's employees than on coffee beans

Starbucks has a secret menu which includes drinks like the:

The Green Eye which contains three shots of espresso
A short size which contains 8 oz. rather than their regular 12 oz. (or tall in Starbucks parlance), the shorter cappuccino is cheaper and more potent and considered by many to taste better.

Dogs and chocolate

Chocolate is toxic for dogs because it contains the compound methylxanthine theobromine, which has a particularly potent effect on dogs and in sufficient quantities can be deadly.

Nose and Ears

Ears and nose continue growing as we age. Ears and nose are made of a plastic-like stuff called cartilage which continues to grow unlike bones which stop growing after puberty.

The Financial Times

In 1893 The Financial Times newspaper turned light salmon pink to distinguish it from the similarly named Financial News. The two rival newspapers merged in 1945 and kept the distinctive colour.

Chinese Take Away

Chinese take away boxes can be unfolded into plates.

Gold

Much of the Earths gold originally came from space. It arrived here when the earth was bombarded by massive meteorite showers about 4 billion years ago.

Buttons

The buttons on men's clothes are on the right side because men have always tended to dress themselves and most men are right-handed.

The buttons on women's clothes are on the left side because they would previously have relied on maids to help dress them.

Dubai International Airport

Dubai International Airport has the most international passengers of any airport in the world.

Butler versus Valet

A butler is the head servant, usually in charge of the kitchen and the dining room whereas a valet is a personal servant, traditional responsible for a gentleman and his dress.

No pants subway ride/No trousers on the Tube

No Pants Subway Ride/No trousers on the Tube is an annual event held in January in which transit passengers ride trains without wearing pants/trousers.

Napoleon Dynamite

The actor Jon Heder who plays 16-year-old Napoleon Dynamite was 27 when the movie was made.

Hidden bear

Hidden in the mountain in the logo of the Toblerone chocolate bar is a bear. The name Bern in Switzerland, which is the hometown of Toblerone, translates as "City of Bears".

Fighting fire with fire

Reactive armour is a type of vehicle armour that reacts in some way to the impact of a weapon to reduce the damage done to the vehicle being protected. Explosive Reactive armour consists of a sheet or slab of high explosive sandwiched between two plates, typically of metal. When a projectile hits it detonates and lessens the damage.

AirBNB

Brian Chesky and Joe Gebbia created the initial concept for Air Bed and Breakfast during the Industrial Design Conference held in San Francisco. At the time, roommates Chesky and Gebbia could not afford the rent for their loft in San Francisco so they made their living room into a bed and breakfast, accommodating three guests on air mattresses and providing homemade breakfast. In March 2009, the name Airbedandbreakfast.com was shortened to Airbnb.com, and the site's content expanded to shared spaces in a variety of properties including entire homes and apartments, private rooms, castles, boats, manors, tree houses, tipis, igloos, private islands, etc.

Barcodes

The first barcodes were used in an industrial context on the sides of railroad rolling stock. Barcodes became commercially successful when they were used to automate supermarket checkout systems, a task for which they have now become almost universal. The very first scanning of the now ubiquitous Universal Product Code (UPC) barcode was on a pack of Wrigley Company chewing gum in June 1974.

Las Vegas

Casinos use many sneaky tricks to keep gamblers from losing interest and wanting to leave. These include:
Not having clocks or windows so that the passage of time goes unnoticed,
Labyrinth like designs, which make it hard to find an exit
Garishly patterned carpet on the casino floor
and pumping in oxygen to make gamblers feel less fatigued.

Classical music

Classical music has been found to increase wine sales revenue in wine stores, but rather than increasing the amount of wine purchased, customers select more expensive wines.

Cows produce more milk when classical music is played for them while they are being milked.

Teenager

Sounds of a particular frequency have been used to dissuade teenagers from congregating in certain areas. The selected sounds are audible to teenagers but not to adults (whose hearing deteriorates as they get older)

Scotched

Johnnie Walker Black Label was the #1 selling Scotch whiskey in Japan. The company wanted to increase the sales volume so they lowered the price expecting that sales would increase but instead, sales plummeted.

In Japan, lists are produced of the Top 10 in each category by price. Johnny Walker used hold the #1 spot for Scotch but the price reduction dropped the scotch down the list and also lowered the social status of giving or receiving Johnnie Walker Black Label as a gift.

When they raised prices their Scotch reverted to the top of the list and so did sales.

Countries that don't use the metric system

Only three countries worldwide don't use the metric system namely Liberia, Myanmar and the United States.

Critical Conversion

NASA lost a $125 million Mars orbiter in 1999 because a Lockheed Martin engineering team used imperial units of measurement while NASA's team used metric ones.

Jedi Library

The Long Room in Trinity College Dublin served as the inspiration for the Jedi Library from the Star Wars films. It was also for a long period the home to the Book of Kells.

Swastika

Historically the Swastika was a sign representing peace and harmony. It's meaning was only subverted in the 20th century.

Peregrine Falcon

One of the world's most widespread raptors, the Peregrine Falcon is renowned for the extreme speed of their hunting stoop (downward swoop). This diving manoeuvre makes them the fastest animal in the world, reaching speeds of over 300 kilometres per hour when they swoop down on their prey.

Soap opera

A soap opera, or soap, is a serial drama for television or radio, whose storylines deal with the lives of multiple characters. The stories in these series typically focus heavily on emotional relationships to the point of melodrama.

The name soap opera stems from the fact that many of the sponsors and producers of the original dramatic serials' broadcast on radio were soap manufacturers, such as Dial Corporation, Procter & Gamble, Colgate-Palmolive and Lever Brothers.

Procter & Gamble even has a separate entertainment division that focuses on creating original content that showcases its brands and products.

Tennis rackets

Tennis rackets were once solely made with with strings spun from cow guts.

To this day these are still favoured by many of the world's top tennis players. The same process is used to produce gut strings for harps and other early instruments.

Zedonkulous

A zedonk is the offspring of a male zebra and a female donkey.

Fire engine red

Fire engines were traditionally red as this was thought to be the colour that stood out most but recent scientific studies have shown that white and yellow are the easiest colours to see at high speeds and red and grey the hardest to make out.

Handgun

The first incidence of a fatal shooting accident was in 1519 when a woman in Welton near Hull in the United Kingdom was accidentally killed by a handgun.

Convenience stores

Most convenience stores profits come from selling soft drinks, similarly filling stations often make as much from selling one soda or soft drink as they do from selling a whole tank of fuel.

Longest echo

The longest verifiable echo lasted for 112 seconds after a gunshot in the Inchindown oil storage tanks, an underground fuel depot constructed during World War II.

The tanks designed to hold 25.5 million litres of fuel were excavated out of solid rock between 1939 and 1941, the tanks were dug deep into the hillside amid concerns about the strengthening of Germany's armed forces and the threat posed by their long-range bombers.

Strangest currency

The Island of Yap in Micronesia in the West Pacific has a very unusual currency called the Rai.

Unlike the small coins in general use around the world theirs are much larger and instead of being made with precious metals are made of stone with a hole in the middle.

The small denomination ones are quite portable but the higher denomination stones are far bigger and not really portable. A British sailor wrote in the late nineteenth century of a stone wheel that was four and a half tons in weight and more than three metres in diameter.

Wikipedia

Wikipedia is the 5th busiest site on the internet.

Parliamentary Bars

As you might expect from a country with a strong drinking tradition the Irish Parliament (Dáil Éireann) has an onsite bar. Not to be outdone the Palace of Westminster home to the House of Commons (the lower house of Parliament of the United Kingdom) has a total of four:

- The Strangers' Bar
- The Members' Smoking Room
- The Pugin Room
- Moncrieff's (named after a particularly hard drinking political pundit)

Rickrolling

Rickrolling is an Internet meme involving the music video for the 1987 song "Never Gonna Give You Up" performed by Rick Astley

A hyperlink is provided which is seemingly relevant to the topic at hand, but actually leads to Astley's video. The link can be masked or obfuscated in some manner so that the user cannot determine the true destination of the link without clicking. If a user falls for the trick they are said to have been rickrolled.

Though the song had been played over 95 million times Astley does not benefit as much as the writer of the song.

Lawyers

Dewey, Cheatem & Howe is the gag name of a fictional law or accounting firm, used in several parody settings.

Tom and Ray Magliozzi, of NPR's Car Talk radio program, named their business corporation "Dewey, Cheetham & Howe". Their corporate offices are located on a third-floor office at the corner of Brattle and JFK Streets in Harvard Square in Cambridge, Massachusetts.

Pi

Piphilology comprises the creation and use of mnemonic techniques to remember a span of digits of the mathematical constant π. The word is a play on the word "pi" itself and of the linguistic field of philology.

A simple mnemonic "How I wish I could determine of circle round the exact relation Archimedes found" gives Pi to 10 places.

Eating one's own dogfood

To eat one's own dogfood is the term used to describe the practice of using one's own product or service. It originated in software companies.

Coke

In the South of the United States all carbonated drinks including Pepsi are referred to as Coke.

Coca-Cola has a product portfolio of more than 3,500 beverages (and 500 brands), spanning from sodas to energy drinks to soy-based drinks.

Coke uses 17% of the annual supply of aluminium in the United Stare

A can of regular Coke sinks in water, whereas a can of diet Coke floats.

Coca-Cola is the number 1 selling soft drink in most markets in the world, except for Scotland where the local concoction Irn Bru comes out on top and parts of the Middle East where Pepsi is the market leader.

Coke has different formulations for different parts of the world, for example in Mexico cane sugar is used whereas the US where high-fructose corn syrup is used as a sweetener
the formulation sold in Saudi Arabia is saltier to suit local tastes.

Coca-Cola has always claimed only two senior executives know the formula at any given time, although they have never revealed names or positiors and according to an advertising campaign these two executives can't travel on the same plane.

Hoover flights

In August 1992 Hoover in the United Kingdom launched a free flights promotion. A consumer needed to spend just £100 on any Hoover product to get two free return flights. However, the company massively underestimated consumer's willingness to navigate a maze of small print where free flights were at stake. Ultimately the company spent £50 million on a promotion that generated just £30m of sales and far less than this of profit.

Business pioneers

The pornography industry has pioneered many technological breakthroughs or at the very least popularised them.

The success of VHS over Betamax was in part attributed to JVC's welcoming attitude towards adult content on VHS.

Other technologies that owe at least some of their success to the adult entertainment industry include moveable type, photography, paperback books, the Minitel, CD-ROMs, pay TV, premium phone numbers, etc.

Chinese inventions

The Chinese invented paper, the compass, gunpowder and printing.

Minitel

The Minitel was a French online service accessible through telephone lines, and is considered one of the world's most successful pre-World Wide Web online services.

It was rolled out experimentally in 1978 in Brittany and throughout France in 1982 by the French Poste, Téléphone et Télécommunications.

It allowed its users to make purchases online, reserve trains, check stock prices, search the telephone directory, communicate via mail, and chat in real time.

Teletext

Teletext was a poor mans internet. Simple text-based information like news, weather, TV schedules and subtitle (or closed captioning) information was transmitted within the television signal
.

The first test transmissions were made by the BBC in 1973, and the service was known as Ceefax ("see facts"). The popularity of World Wide Web ultimately lead to it's demise with the BBC ceasing broadcast of teletext in 2012.

Modena

The area in and around Modena in Italy has been given the name Supercar valley due to being home to the majority of the world's supercar production. Lamborghini and Maserati are based in Modena itself with Ferrari is based nearby in Maranello.

Laconic Wit

Philip II of Macedon the father of the great conqueror Alexander the Great once tried to intimidate the state of Sparta which was renowned for it's military strength. He sent a message "You are advised to submit without further delay, for if I bring my army on your land, I will destroy your farms, slay your people and raze your city."

The Spartans replied simply with a one-word response to Philip: "If."

Philip never attempted to conquer Sparta and the term "Laconic wit," was named for the Spartan region of Laconia.

First airline

Deutsche Luftschiffahrts-AG (DELAG) was the the first revenue generating airline, it flew airships though rather than airplanes. By 1914 it had carried over 34,000 passengers on over 1,500 flights.

Desire Lines

A desire line is a path created along the shortest or most easily navigated route between an origin and destination.

Desire lines emerge as shortcuts where the constructed ways take a circuitous route, or have gaps, or are lacking entirely.

Several universities in the US built buildings first and after the desire lines were made went on to build the paths / sidewalks.

Zeppelin

Zeppelin dirigibles were rigid airships filled with balloons containing gases that were lighter than air. These balloons were made from cow intestines. The construction of a single dirigible required intestines of literally hundreds of thousands of cattle.

The demand for these collagen balloons resulted in the ban of consumption of sausage in Germany during WWI as all butchers in Germany as well as occupied nations were required to supply all intestines to the state.

The Art Deco spire of the Empire State Building was originally, if impractically, designed to serve as a mooring mast for Zeppelins and other airships to dock at.

Special Forces

Special Forces are highly trained military units tasked with carrying out unconventional, often high-risk missions. Special forces, emerged in the early 20th century, with a significant growth in the field during the Second World War.

The SAS and SBS are special forces from the United Kingdom.

The Spetsnaz were the special forces of the former Soviet Union. They were infamous for their extremely tough and often brutal training. To complete training candidates had to prevail in one on one combat against a number of already qualified Spetsnaz soldiers.

As the country with the largest military spending it is no surprise that the United States has both many different special forces and large numbers of them. Among the most commonly known are the Navy Seals and Delta Force.

CIA - Intel

Oddly the CIA shares a few characteristics with Intel the semiconductor manufacturer. CIA officers trained at "The Farm" wear blue badges as do Intel full time employees, contractors at both wear green badges.

Intel's main manufacturing plants are located predominantly in the US with a base in Europe, (Ireland) and the Middle East (Israel) but they have sales offices worldwide)

The reticle technology used in the manufacturing of the latest generation of microprocessors is also that used in spy satellites to resolve detail from the ground underneath.

China Syndrome

"China Syndrome" is the fanciful term used to describe a fictional worst-case scenario nuclear meltdown, where reactor components melt through their containment structures and into the underlying earth, "all the way to China."

On the 16th of March 1979 a film of the same name was released. Its plot revolved around a television reporter and her cameraman who discover safety cover ups at a nuclear power plant. The film release was met with a severe backlash from the nuclear power industry's who decried it as being "sheer fiction" and a "character assassination of an entire industry.

Just 12 days later the Three Mile Island nuclear accident occurred in Dauphin County, Pennsylvania.

The Chernobyl disaster came close to an actual China Syndrome or containment breach.

Steven Spielberg

Steven Spielberg dropped out of college in 1968. He was only a few credits short of a diploma. So in 2002, after winning 3 Oscars, 5 honorary doctorates, and 2 lifetime achievement awards, he returned to California State University, Long Beach, to complete a degree in film and electronic arts. He passed FEA 309, the advanced filmmaking class. To demonstrate his proficiency in filmmaking, he had submitted Schindler's List.

Complete colour blindness

Some people are completely colour-blind i.e. they cannot tell the difference between colours at all. They see only in terms of light and dark. This condition is called achromatopsia.

Hotel versus Motel

The main difference between a motel and a hotel is that rooms are entered internally from within the hotel whereas motel rooms allow the guest to drive up to or near the door of the room. It is also a portmanteau of motoring and hotel.

Cinemas and candy

Cinemas make most if not all of their profits from the food and drink they sell to cinema goers. This explains the emphasis on food and drink in cinema foyers.

Interesting University Courses

Theme Park Engineer at California State University Long Beach

Bowling Industry Management and Technology at Vincennes University

Puppetry at the University of Connecticut

Floriography

The Victorians used flowers as a means of clandestine communication. This language is called floriography. In Harry Potter the very first potion Snape asks Harry's class to complete contains a reference encoded in this manner.

Elvis

Elvis never gave an encore

Snopes

With the risk in the usage of the internet comes a new phenomenon, the internet rumour. And with the rise in the internet rumour come the websites that seek to debunk them. Of these the most popular is the website Snopes which is run by a husband and wife team. It exists with the purpose of determining the veracity of claims on the internet.

Stock imagery

Much of the imagery used in advertising is stock imagery used over and over again.

Police

The first professional police were introduced by Sir Robert Peel in The United Kingdom when he became Home Secretary in 1822. The government at the time didn't want them to be mistaken for a military force, so they were unarmed and had completely different uniforms.

Electronic Dance Music

The tempo in beats per minute of electronic dance music tends to match the heartbeat of the dancers so most dance music tends to have a tempo between 120 and 140 beats per minute.

Subliminal messages

The horror film The Exorcist is well known for its frightening yet effective use of subliminal images throughout the film, depicting a white-faced demon named Captain Howdy. This image is shown in the character Father Karras' nightmare, where it flashes across the screen for a few seconds before fading away

No river

Madrid is the only European capital city not built on a river.

Wind and rain

Though most people think of Ireland being synonymous with rain, they wouldn't straight away think of it as being windy. However, for a period of time on Christmas Eve in 2016 68% of all electricity consumed in Ireland was produced from wind energy.

Taking the piss

To know when to mate, a male giraffe will continuously head-butt the female in the bladder until she urinates. The male then tastes the pee and that helps it determine whether the female is ovulating.

Names

Many countries have strict rules around naming children, some of them even enforce it by law.

In Germany names must be approved by the local registration office, called Standesamt, the first name must be consistent with the gender of the child and the name chosen must not negatively affect the well-being of the child.

Denmark also provides a list of pre-approved names. If parents in Denmark want to choose a name that is not on the list, they must get special permission from their church and have it reviewed by the Ankestyrelsen. Some names that are not permitted in Denmark are Anus, Pluto and Monkey.

World's biggest hotel

Prora the world's largest hotel is located on the sea island of Ruegen a Baltic sea resort in Germany. It has 10,000 rooms, all sea facing rooms. The resort was constructed between 1936 and 1939 on Adolf Hitler's instructions.

XJ220 Transit Van

A much talked about concept among motoring aficionados is the idea of a stealth or sleeper vehicle. Something with high performance wrapped up in sheep's clothing. One vehicle that surely qualifies is the Jaguar XJ220 powered Ford Transit Van. The XJ220 the tested incognito by acquiring a Ford Transit van and fitted it with the XJ220's engine and running gear. The 542 bhp engine made for a very fast and powerful van with few tell-tale signs.

Toyota Corolla

The Toyota Corolla is the worlds best selling car, it was also arguably one of the most boring. Toyota did however revolutionise car manufacturing with it's Toyota Production System. TPS is also known as lean production.

Lean production has several key components such as kaizen workshops where frontline workers meet to solve production problems; kanban, a scheduling system for just-in-time production; and the andon cord, which, can pulled by any worker at any time, causing the production line to stop so that an issue can be fixed immediately.

Games console

Apple at one stage developed and sold a games console called the Pippin. The name comes from a varietal of apple. The Pippin was not a commercial success, partly due to it's inability to support internet browsing a nascent but key technology at the time.

TP-82

The TP-82 pistol was a triple-barrelled Soviet firearm that was carried by cosmonauts on space missions. It was intended as a survival aid to be used after landings and before recovery in the Siberian wilderness. The pistol could be used for hunting, to defend against predators and for visible and audible distress signals. The detachable butt stock was also a machete that came with a canvas sheath.

Ki

When practitioners of karate make a noise it is for a number of reason, one of which is to intimidate their opponent another reason is to try and create a sound with the same natural frequency as their opponent's internal organs which when delivered with a blow would potentially cause their opponents internal organs to disintegrate.

Mexico / US

All the states with the highest number of Spanish speakers were the ones that the US won from Mexico after the Mexican American War.

Angled Mouse Pointer

When the Window Icon Mouse Pointer graphical user interface was developed by Xerox, the vertical mouse pointer was very difficult to see against the background due to the low resolution displays of the time. To make it easier to see a choice was made to rotate it 45 degrees rather than making it larger. Even though screens today are of a much higher resolution the pointer remains as it was.

Planned Obsolescence

In the 1920s the fledgling automobile industry was faced with it's first decline in sales. Supply had caught up with demand and anyone who could afford a car had bought one.

To combat this sales decline Alfred P. Sloan, president of General Motors introduced the concept of a new model for each calendar year. Often the changes were more of a cosmetic nature and less technological breakthroughs. The idea that something that worked perfectly would be made obsolete just because a new model looked different revolutionised the automobile industry.

IBM company culture

IBM is one of the largest and most influential computer companies in the world. It had a unique corporate culture, which was heavily employee centric long before it was popular to be so, one unusual manifestation of this was the company songs, which their employees had to learn and sing together. Another was it's earlier focus on inclusion and lack of discrimination in it's workforce. It was also highly innovative with key IBM inventions including the ATM, the barcode and DRAM (memory on a chip), RISC (Reduced Instruction Set Computing)

Alcohol dehydrogenase

Alcohol dehydrogenases are a group of dehydrogenase enzymes that humans and other animals use to break down alcohols that are toxic to their hosts. Many Asian people have a genetic variation that means they have less of them and this variation affects their ability to metabolise alcohol.

Oranges

Not all oranges are orange due to the fact that in warmer climates it doesn't get cold enough to break down the chlorophyll. These oranges are yellow or green when ripe. In some countries these are treated with ethylene to give them the characteristic orange colour consumers associate with the fruit.

Nuclear reactor

Though building the first nuclear reactor was an epic undertaking it has become progressively easier over time to the point where several individuals have built nuclear reactors. Notable among these was David Charles Hahn who at 17 attempted to build a homemade breeder nuclear reactor in a backyard shed at his mother's house in Commerce Township, Michigan in the United States.

Atomic bomb college assignment

In 1976 John Aristotle Phillips an undergraduate at Princeton University designed a nuclear weapon using solely information that was in the public domain. In early 1977, several months after the story first went public, Phillips was contacted by a Pakistani official trying to purchase his bomb design.

INES

The International Nuclear and Radiological Event 7-point Scale was introduced in 1990 by the International Atomic Energy Agency to communicate the magnitude of nuclear accidents similar to the way the Richter scale is used for earthquakes. The Chernobyl disaster and the Fukushima Daiichi disaster both scored the top score of 7 on the INES scale.

Taxing situation

Only two countries in the world tax their citizens based on nationality rather than residence, the United States and Eritrea.

Stock market indices

The Dow Jones Industrial average is a stock market index and was first calculated on the 26th May 1896. Of the original constituents only General Electric is still in todays index, and even it was removed twice and reinstated twice. Large parts of it's current business such as selling and maintaining aircraft engines and financial services didn't even exist a century ago.

Implied Volatility

VIX is a trademarked ticker symbol for the Chicago Board Options Exchange Market Volatility Index, a measure of the implied volatility of S&P 500 index options.

It is often referred to as the fear index.

Semco

Semco SA is a Brazilian company majority owned by Ricardo Semler with a very antithetical corporate philosophy. Semco employees set their own hours, design their own workplace, choose their own computer systems, share all information and have no secrets. There are no job titles, no written policies and no Human Resources department. Employees evaluate their managers and the results of this evaluation are posted publicly. All salaries are public information unless the employee requests that they not be published. Most radically of all employees set their own salaries.

<u>Passwords to avoid</u>

Commonly used passwords that are best avoided include:

The numeric:

123456
1234567
12345678
123456789

The cynical:

trustno1
shadow

The obvious:

password
qwerty

and the cute:

iloveyou
abc123
sunshine

<u>Kindle</u>

Originally the Kindle didn't have page numbers but after user complaints it was restored.

Atari

Steve Jobs and Steve Wozniak both once worked for Atari. And Atari's founder Nolan Bushnell turned down Steve Jobs' offer of a third of Apple for $50,000

MDMA

The first mass-scale production of MDMA for recreational use in the United States came courtesy of the so-called Boston Group, a small contingent of chemists who were tenured professors at MIT and Harvard and who were colleagues of LSD guru Timothy Leary. The Boston Group took it themselves first and then went on to handpick distributors in New York to distribute MDMA at Studio 54 and Paradise Garage. It was touted as a healthier alternative to cocaine.

Chimera

A chimera (also spelled chimaera) is a single organism made up of genetically distinct cells. This can manifest itself in a number of different ways including an organism having male and female organs, two different blood types, or different colour eyes, etc.

The existence of chimerism complicates DNA testing, and has legal implications.

In a number of notable cases women have been accused of not being their children's biological mother after DNA tests apparently showed that their children could not be theirs.

In one case a Lydia Fairchild was charged with fraud and her custody of her children was challenged. An additional DNA test found matching DNA in her cervical tissue and charges against her were dropped.

In another case Karen Keegan, who was also accused of not being sons biological mother. She required a kidney transplant and initial DNA tests gave different results for the mother and son.

Nascar

Stock car racing in the United States has its origins in the Appalachian region during the Prohibition era. The makers of illegal liquor used small fast cars to deliver their product with many drivers modifying their cars to improve performance and handling.

Chicken gun

To ensure that airplanes can withstand the effects of bird strikes airplane manufacturers use large diameter compressed air cannon to fire chicken carcases at the planes windows, engines and fuselage.

These cannon are also used to test the windscreens of high speed trains.

Giant mushroom

The Termitomyces titanicus mushroom is believed to be the largest edible mushroom and can reach almost a metre in diameter.

Rare earth elements

A rare earth metal is one of a set of seventeen chemical elements in the periodic table. They are composed of the fifteen lanthanides plus scandium and yttrium. Scandium and yttrium are considered rare earth elements because they tend to occur in the same ore deposits as the lanthanides and exhibit similar chemical properties.

Though rare they have many important commercial applications including use in Wind turbines and smartphones which contain over 60 elements including small amounts of the rare earth elements.

Hotspot

The Walkie Talkie skyscraper in London was blamed for melting parts of a car parked nearby. It's unusual design acts as a concave mirror and focuses light and heat on a number of nearby car parking spaces with enough strength to melt plastics, etc.

Soda Stream

Guy Gilbey of the London gin distillers, W & A Gilbey Ltd invented an "Apparatus for aerating liquids", in 1903. The device added carbon dioxide from a pressurised cylinder to create soda water also known as carbonated water. It was sold mainly to the upper classes (including the royal household). Flavoured concentrates such as cherry ciderette and sarsaparilla, were introduced in the 1920s. These devices continue to be sold to this day under the Soda Stream brand name.

50-euro note

The 50 euro note uses the rare earth element Europium as a security feature. The stars made with it illuminate under ultraviolet light.

Berlin Tempelhof

Berlin Tempelhof airport was the world's first with an underground railway station.

St. Valentine's heart

Whitefriar Street Carmelite Church in Dublin, Ireland is home to the heart of that incurable romantic St. Valentine.

USS Gerald Ford

The USS Gerald R. Ford and other carriers in it's class will have gender-neutral berthing and no urinals, in a departure from all previous carrier classes.

Giant Sequoia

Giant Sequoia are a species of tree renowned for their heights, girth and age. Examples can grow to over 95 meters high, girths of 47 meters and ages of over 35000 years. Many examples are large enough to drive a car through them.

Juiced

People think of "not from concentrate orange juice" as being a less processed and a more natural choice. However, the production process is one of massive industrialisation. Consistent tasting juice is produced year round though the orange growing season is only 3 months and juice contains over 600 flavours.

First the juice is deoxygenated to prevent it from spoiling but as this diminishes the flavour engineered flavour packs added to make the juice taste fresh. Flavour packs don't have to be listed as an ingredient on the label because technically they are derived from orange essence and oil.

The juice companies hire flavour and fragrance companies, often the same ones that formulate perfumes for Dior and Calvin Klein, to engineer the flavour packs that are added back to the juice to make it taste fresh.

PL-01 Tank

Poland's PL-01 tank has an innovative stealth technology. Most modern weapons system use infrared, so concealing or minimising the infrared signature is one of the the best ways to avoid detection. The PL-01 tank utilises a combination of infrared sensors mounted on the tank that detect its surroundings and then displays which output a pattern on the tank's covering that correspond to those surroundings. The cover can also disguise itself to look like a smaller vehicle like car or another smaller object.

TGV signs

There are some signs on France's high speed TGV network which are only visible at the high speeds at which the train travels.

Marlboro barcode advertising

To attempt to skirt a law that forbids tobacco advertising Marlboro who sponsored the Ferrari Formula 1 team replaced their logo with a barcode. However, at the 320 km/h operating speed of the car the barcode looked a lot like the Marlboro logo. The European Public Health Commissioner objected and told Marlboro that the use of the barcode in this fashion constituted subliminal advertising.

Universal Studios

At Universal Studios in Los Angeles one can find the plane crash scene from War of the Worlds, Wisteria Lane from ABC's hit series Desperate Housewives and the creepy Bates Motel from the film Psycho all next to each other on the back lot at the iconic film studio.

Monsterpark

At Germanys Monsterpark one can drive a selection of over 130 large industrial machines including backhoes, dumpers, industrial loaders, etc. No special licence or experience is required.

Mountain unicycling

Mountain unicycling is an an adventure sport similar to mountain biking except that it is carried out using a unicycle. Mountain unicycling utilises specially designed unicycles with stronger than normal hubs, larger, grippier tires, high grip pedals and stronger frames. Mountain unicycling riders need to possess an enhanced sense of balance and strong core strength.

Beaked whale

The Beaked whale can hold its breath longer and dive deeper than any other animal. The deepest recorded dive was to a depth of over 2,992 meters and the longest lasting breath was over 137 minutes. A human would be crushed by the water pressure at a much lesser depth.

10 and 12

Convention shows watches in advertising with their hands at 10 and 2, this is because logos are typically placed under the 12 and this positioning of the hands shows the logo to the best effect.

Bone china

Bone china known for it's whiteness and translucency does actually have animal bone as an ingredient. It was pioneered by Thomas Frye at his Bow porcelain factory in London in 1748.

Joki

In Jakarta Indonesia Joki hire themselves out as an additional passenger so that drivers have the required number of passengers to use the carpool streets during peak traffic hours.

Tea bags

Tea bags date back to the Tang Dynasty 618 - 690 in China where tea was first preserved in paper, folded and sewn into square bags. Their commercial introduction dates back to the early 20th century in the US while Tetley introduced tea bags to the United Kingdom in 1953.

Supercharger vs Turbocharger

Both turbochargers and superchargers are forced induction systems which compress the air flowing into an engine to increase performance,

Turbocharger get their power from the exhaust stream whereas a supercharger gets its power from a belt that connects directly to the engine. It gets its power the same way that the water pump or alternator does.

A turbocharger is more efficient than a supercharger because it is using the wasted energy in the exhaust stream for its power source.

<u>Fast</u>

The turbines in turbochargers can rotate at over 280,000 rpm

<u>Diesel</u>

The diesel engine is named after the German inventor and mechanical engineer Rudolph Diesel who died in suspicious circumstances.

<u>KLF</u>

Bill Drummond and Jimmy Cauty founders of Stadium house group KLF were known for their unusual stunts and tricks. Some of these included deleting their back catalogue and burning a million pounds sterling.

<u>Eastman Kodak</u>

Eastman Kodak was the iconic film producer which had a virtual stranglehold on the camera and film industry until the onset of the digital photography age.

Eastman Kodak's founder was among the first American companies to employ a full time research scientist and thus starting the concept of research and development as a core competency and differentiator for companies.

Its name was chosen by it's founder George Eastman who had a fondness for the letter K.

<u>Classical music riot</u>

Though Classical music is often associated with peace and serenity there have been a number of occasions where performances have been an incitement to violence and even riots.

Shukhov Tower

The Shukhov Tower is a 160-meter-high free-standing steel diagrid structure stands a few kilometers south of the Kremlin in Moscow. It was built in 1920 - 1922 during the Russian Civil War. It was conceived as a radio mast so high that it could broadcast to far away Soviet territories.

7-year Scholarship

Oxfords All Souls College is famous for its 'Examination Fellowship'.

The 7 years long fellowship includes a stipend, fellow status with voting rights at All Souls, and open access to conduct research at the college with no worry of accountability of work or research for 7 years.

The lucky candidates get seven years to research in ideal conditions, in regular contact with leading scholars in their field, and free from many of the pressures, financial and otherwise, which normally afflict graduate students.

Hakone turnpike

Japan's answer to Germany's Nurburgring is the Hakone turnpike. It offers a unique driving experience on a closed section of road rising from just above sea level to 1011 m. Though it does have speed limits these are more honoured in the breach than in the observance.

Joan of Arc

Joan of Arc rose from being a peasant girl to a highly effective military leader but when captured by the English they saw just the peasant and severely underestimated her intellect.

A key example of this was her trial she was asked if she knew she was in God's grace. The question was an ecclesiastical trap as Church doctrine at the time held that no one could be sure of being in God's grace.

If Joan had answered yes, then she would have convicted of heresy and if she had answered no, then it would have been an admission of her own guilt.

Instead she answered: 'If I am not, may God put me there; and if I am, may God so keep me.'

Fruit Roll-ups

The food company General Mills had to amend it's packaging after a California woman Annie Lam took a case against them. Their product Strawberry Naturally Flavored Fruit Roll-Ups contain no strawberries but are instead made with among other things pear concentrate, corn syrup, dried corn syrup, sugar and partially hydrogenated cottonseed oil.

As a result of the case General Mills has to meet two conditions:

1) The label can't show images of strawberries if the product doesn't contain strawberries
2) The actual percentage of fruit must be listed if the product's label carries the claim "Made with Real Fruit,"

Vibrator

The vibrator has an unusual history. Doctors used to treat some women for hysteria by pelvic massage aka masturbation and the vibrator was invented to make this task less onerous for the doctors in question.

Caffeine

Caffeine helps the body absorb medications faster and can increase the effectiveness of many drugs. This is why many over the counter drugs contain caffeine as an ingredient.

Self surgeon

In 1961 Dr Leonid Rogozov left Leningrad on the 6th Soviet Antarctic

Expedition. Rogozov was the sole doctor and he had additional responsibilities as an assistant meteorologist and heavy vehicle operator.

On the 29th April 1961 Rogozov started having pain in his lower right portion of the abdomen, his condition worsened and he diagnosed himself as having acute appendicitis.

Due to the remote location and extreme weather airlifting in a surgical team was impossible so instead Rogozov operated on himself taking an hour and 45 minutes to cut himself open and remove his appendix.

Within two weeks of his operation Rogozov was back at work and he completed his full year stay in Antarctica returning home with the rest of his team.

Ewoks

Ewoks speak a hybrid of Tibetan and Nepalese

Fastest speeding ticket

A Texas driver of a Koenigsegg CC was given a speeding ticket for driving at 242 miles per hour.

Justice Prisoner and Alien Transportation System

The Justice Prisoner and Alien Transportation System nicknamed Conair is the airline for flying convicts in United States

Pet Food

Marks & Spencer, a middle class high street retailer employs a pet food taster. Simon Allison's official title is a senior food technologist with special responsibility for pet food.

He spits rather than swallows the pet food due to the negative health implications (food that is suitable for dogs and cats is not suitable for humans and vice versa)

Stock Ticker symbols

Companies on the stock market are uniquely identified by stock or ticker symbols. These consist of letters, numbers or a combination of both. Some companies choose these to make a word or acronym that fits in with their business. Examples include:

Cedar Fair Entertainment Company, which operates large amusement parks in the United States, uses "FUN" as its symbol,

Steinway Musical Instruments uses the symbol "LVB", to honour composer and pianist Ludwig van Beethoven.

Harley-Davidson uses "HOG" named for its Harley Owners Group.

Sotheby's (the famous auction house) uses the symbol "BID".

Cheesecake Factory uses the the ticker symbol CAKE

Winglets

Winglets are the devices at the wing tip that serve to improve the aerodynamic efficiency of aircraft. This work by reducing the aircraft's drag. Wingtip devices effectively increase the aspect ratio of a wing without increasing the wingspan. They are fitted to the Airbus A380 so that they can be used on existing runaways and taxiways without the need to widen them. They are also used by some airlines to advertise their websites.

Edwin Harris Dunning

Edwin Harris Dunning was the first pilot to land an airplane on a moving ship. Unfortunately, he was killed five days later, during a subsequent landing attempt when he was knocked unconscious and he drowned in the cockpit before he could be rescued.

Coincidence

Just before D-Day, 5 of the top-secret code names were answers in the Daily Telegraph crosswords compiled by Leonard Dawes the headmaster at Strand school in Effingham, Surrey. Dawe arrested by MI5 but it was determined that he had heard the words from boys at the school, who had in turn overheard them from soldiers.

Notable escape from East Germany

There were many notable escape attempts from East to West Germany but one of the most dramatic escapes was carried out by the Strelczyk and Wetzel families who fled to the West in a homemade hot air balloon.

Hans Strelczyk a mechanic and Gunter Wetzel a mason fashioned burners for the balloon using old propane cylinders and their wives made a balloon from scraps of canvas and old bed sheets.
On the 16th of September 1979, the two families floated over the border to freedom. The story was immortalised in a Disney movie called Night Crossing.

Iron man

The Iron man competition came about after athletes debated which discipline lead to the fittest overall athlete. The debate was settled by them competing in a race combining three existing long-distance competitions in Hawaii namely the Waikiki Roughwater Swim 3.86 km. the Around-Oahu Bike Race 185.07 km and the Honolulu Marathon 42.195 km.

Gordon Haller, a US Navy Communications Specialist, was the first to earn the title Ironman by completing the course in a time of 11 hours, 46 minutes, 58 seconds.

Dog food

The Pet food market in the Unites States is worth an estimated $23 billion.

Supermarket's sneaky tricks

Supermarket design makes use of many subtle tricks to entice shoppers to buy more right from the time they enter until they leave, and to buy higher margin goods.

First as shoppers enter a warm blast of air relaxes and welcomes you (or cold in hot climates) Next feature is a clear zone just inside the door, to give shopper a few seconds of relaxation.

When shoppers enter a store, they naturally turn to their dominant side which for ~80% of them is to the right. So this is where stores locate the offers and non food items like clothes, toys, DVDs, CDs and increasingly nowadays electrical and electronic goods.

Supermarkets use smells like roasting chicken, freshly baked bread, or freshly ground coffee beans to encourage shoppers. The bread though usually arrives frozen and partially baked and is simply finished off in store. Free samples are given out not to sell more product but simply to whet a shopper's appetite.

If a supermarket can keep shoppers in the store longer then they will spend more money, so often they play slow relaxing music, this encourages you to walk slowly through the store and buy more. Playing classical music in the wine section to boost sales.

Prepared vegetables and salad which are a way of marking up the cost by several hundred percent.

Supermarket chains and their suppliers use buy one get one free promotions to unload excess stock, maintain brand loyalty and shift the cost of maintaining inventory from the supplier / supermarket to the homeowner.

Products at eye level come to our attention more so this is where the most expensive, highest margin products are stocked. This is adjusted for men, women and particularly children where sugary cereals, snacks and junk are placed at their eye level. This technique is also used in the DVD section, with children's movies at their eye level.

Known value items such as bread, butter, milk and sugar are sold below cost to lure customers from smaller stores. Then they make it up by raising the price on all the other products. These same items are at the back of the store so you have to walk through the whole store to get to them and probably pick up a few things you don't need!

Fruit and vegetables are put at the start of the typical store to make you feel virtuous about your shopping choices. Similarly, alcohol and snack foods are generally put in the last few aisles so that as you have bought lots of good healthy food it is easier to splurge, plus by this stage you are tired and feel like you deserve a reward.

Loyalty cards, are used to gather information about shopping habits. Research has found that loyalty card holders buy more groceries and travel greater distances to buy them.
Often the resulting discount vouchers are for products you wouldn't normally buy.

Supermarkets regularly rearrange their stores so shoppers walk around more searching for items they usually buy and end up buying more things they hadn't planned to buy.

Themed displays or aisles like barbecues in summer. Valentines day. Easter, Halloween. Christmas. Sporting events. Are all setup to boost sales.

Sweets and magazines are generally located at the checkout within reach of both adults and children.

The simplest defence against all of this is to plan your meals, shop on and full stomach and shop with a list and stick to it!

<u>Comments & corrections</u>

If you believe that anything in this book is inaccurate or plain wrong, I'd love to hear from you at:

thewriteriswrong@gmail.com